© Copyright 2011 Jelani Faraja Kafela

All rights reserved. This book is protected under the copyright laws of the United States of America. No portion of this book may be reproduced in any form, without the written permission of the publisher. Permission granted on request.

Unlock Publishing House
231 West Hampton Place
Capitol Heights, MD 20743
www.unlockpublishinghouse.com
1 (240) 619-3852

Cover Design: J. F. Kafela
Page Layout and Editing: Rosita Dozier

*Unlock Publishing House is not responsible
for any content or determination of work. All information is solely considered as
the point of view of the author*

ISBN: 978-0-9838982-8-3

Table of Contents

PREFACE ix

INTRODUCTION:

Part A: Follow One Course Until Successful! 13

PART B: Faith-Obedience-
Commitment-Unity Servant-hood 31

FOCUS:

Enjoying the Grace;
Extending the Glory; Establishing the Throne 55

Stretch out 63

The Treasure of Incredible Worth 71

Giving Your Heart A Home! 81

Till Death Do Us Part Or Until I'm Tired of Trying 93

"Excuse Me, But Your Integrity is Showing!" 103

"Entering the Promise Dimension" 113

A Covenant of Trust 123

Choices You Make, Chances You Take! 141

"Who Do People Say That I Am?" 155

A Season of Consecration as Chosen Vessels 167

CONCLUSION 189

PREFACE

Jesus said, "Where your treasure is, there will your heart be also," Matthew 6.21. So then, it seems that where your heart is, you will also find your focus...

We live in a world full of distractions. If you're someone who has limited energy, it's all too easy to let your creative ambitions slide. There are plenty of life's day-to-day activities that, if we let them can easily take up all our limited time or energy. If you want to lead a creative life, or even make your living from your creative endeavors, then you'll need to learn to focus on and prioritize your important work. Focus isn't easy, especially if you spend a significant amount of your time feeling overwhelmed. But the good news is focus is a habit you can learn, and sustain creatively and spiritually; focus can often be energizing.

We are repeatedly told that in the business environment focus is essential to success. But when it comes to things that have to do with our spirituality we don't focus particularly well. It might be useful to explain a bit of the science behind why focus is important. And don't worry, I'm not qualified to tell you anything other than you get what you focus on – well, at least that is my opinion anyway.

A professor of Psychology and Management concluded in a recent report that we have available to us through our senses around 2 million 'bits' of information per second. Reports say that we can only process a certain amount of information at any given time. If we were simultaneously conscious of all the data coming at us, we'd go insane trying to process it all and stay focused. So, according to these studies, these 'bits' of information are filtered by our subconscious, through three main mechanisms:

> We "Delete" - what's not of immediate importance or relevance
>
> We "Distort" - what doesn't fit our paradigm, until it does
>
> We "Generalize" - it into things that we can recognize

In this modern age it's so difficult to focus on what is important. It's not entirely our fault. For the last few generations the television and other sensory mediums have told us to want everything. Then the Internet gave us infinite options. It's no wonder anyone can concentrate on their spiritual needs when their emotions, feelings and thinking is so bombarded everyday through all the sensory mediums touching our lives. (i.e., Facebook, Twitter, Cable T.V. iPods, iPads, cell phones, reality programming etc.)

Why focus when you can spend all day hitting the refresh button? Why focus spiritually or meditate on biblical principles when our natural senses are so stimulated and overworked by the sensory mediums controlling our consciousness 24/7/365?

It's important to take time to remember how to focus. The most successful people in the world seem to realize that in order to create anything meaningful, they need to turn it all off and focus in narrowly consigned ways for success. They focus on that which is most important to their success. In order to do anything that matters, you need to cultivate a healthy atmosphere of complete focus in order to make a difference in your own life and change the world. Marianne Williamson's says: "it is important to understand that your playing small doesn't serve the world." I might add, "What you don't focus on, you diminish your likelihood of impacting the world."

We use the acronym FOCUS to represent a Sincere Theological Faith. FOCUS: faith -obedience– commitment – unity and servant-hood is a way to pinpoint our theology for success in our Christian walk and service. It does not serve us to play small and live unfocused as Christians. Focus is actually an acronym, and is more than just a word! I also learned this from Donald Trump (**F**ollow **o**ne **c**ourse **u**ntil **s**uccessful) and this helps to guide our thinking while our previous acronym guides our actions.

INTRODUCTION

Part A: Follow One Course Until Successful!

The Bible says, 'Because strait is the gate, and narrow is the way, which leads to life, and few there be that find it." (Mt 7:14). The way is straight and narrow: we must pass through this rough way and suffer, endure, change and so enter into life. It is best entered with a focused attitude and approach. With the Bible as your primary textbook and the Holy Spirit as the guiding influence, you will find yourself encouraged to know and use your spiritual gifts as you follow God's will for your life.

Our experience is that continually learning to employ God's Word and God's perspectives as focused development of our spiritual theology enhances our relationship with God. The consequences of this affects how we offer our surrendered hearts in worship, share our lives together in stewardship, shape our lives and ministries in servant-hood, and synergize our evangelistic efforts interdependently as we serve our divine purposes. This means we focus our lives and ministries on the Savior as significant and eternal – both for us and for those we impact.

See how simple it is now? FOCUS is now a very powerful word, which can guide our thinking and from that guide our actions. It tells you exactly what you need to do for success. And it is so versatile you can use it to successfully accomplish what you are thinking.

You can FOCUS on your goals, or the actions to accomplish fulfillment and greater joy in following Christ enjoying the life of faith through focus. All you have to do is concentrate on one way of getting to where you want to be and then follow that course until you are successful.

WHY FOCUS IS IMPORTANT FOR SUCCESS?

If you are a teacher who wants to ignite the minds of the next generation, then you will not have as much success in real estate as one who knows nothing about igniting minds. Knowing yourself and expressing yourself in your goals is to prioritize your goals and focus. Each individual has a limited amount of time in their day. Since that is always the case, expect that if you want to excel at any particular thing, or in any particular niche, you need to have a narrow focus. "Strait is the way and narrow is the gate."

Spiritually, we can get caught up in trying to be all things at once because our theology focus blurs our thinking and our unfocused gifting for ministry diminishes our successful approach to serving God. Too many of us are unfocused in our approach to ministry and life. We focus more on what others think we should have, instead of maximizing through focus, what we do have and what God wants for us.

At the end of the day our theology and ministry approaches are formed more by sensory media than by spiritual meditation, preparation, prayer, partnerships and participation synergistically in the priesthood of all believers.

Proverbs 20:27 says, "The Lord's light penetrates the human spirit, exposing every hidden motive." The Bible is not for us to increase our knowledge but to change our lives, becoming more like Christ. The Bible must be our standard of influence, our compass in directing our life's transactions. It becomes our advice for all the choices we make. It needs to be the standard for assessing everything that has to do with my life.

For many they base their decisions by four ways: the culture (everybody is doing it), Traditions ((that is the way it has always been done), Rationale (what seems most reasonable), Emotions (How I feel at the moment). Not that these are wrong in many areas of what we need to do but they have been distorted by the fall in the garden thus negatively can affect our focus.

We need something that will be a perfect standard. It is the Bible that says in Proverbs 30:5 "Every word of God is pure." 2 Tim. 3:16 informs us, "All scripture is given by inspiration of God, and is profitable for doctrine, for reproof, for correction, for instruction in righteousness."

We need to ask first in all our decisions, what does the Bible say?" When we discover what the Word says, we must act on it whether it makes sense to us or if we feel like it or not. It is easy for one to come with a clogged mind, shallow mind, preoccupied mind and miss what God wants to say to us. If we are not learning from the message we need to recheck our attitude. It is when we come with a humble and approachable mind that God is able to speak to us.

Our spirits are God's contact point through which God illuminates us and brings His true nature into focus. It is the Holy Spirit, which is the Lord's light, then guides us into the truth so we can focus our influence where God has designed and sent us.

Many come into ministry excited but unfocused leading to burnout when they attempt to take on too many things. We simply become frustrated by taking on ministry activities for which we are not designed for. Without focus we cannot effectively accomplish the mission for which God has called us.

A good way to focus is shining our light on four things:

1. Defining mission
2. Focusing your influence
3. Finding your God-given mission
4. Writing a personal mission statement

There is a movie staring Tom Hanks and Ron Howard directs which focuses our attention on the failed Apollo 13 moon walk mission. Apollo 13 was the seventh manned mission in the American Apollo space program and the third with the intention of landing on the Moon. The craft launched on April 11, 1970. They had to abort the landing after the oxygen tank exploded two days later, crippling the service module upon which the Command Module depended. Despite great hardship caused by limited power, loss of cabin heat, shortage of potable water and the critical need to jury-rig the carbon dioxide removal system, the crew returned safely to Earth on April 17.

The movie helps us to focus on the fact that these astronauts are on a mission. But they are not on the mission alone. Everyone at mission control, including their wives and families, are part of the mission as well. You could define their mission as first getting three men to the moon. Once tragedy happens the focus narrows to getting three men home safely. Each person, onboard the space craft or in the command center, has a specific part of the mission to complete. Their focus is entirely on the mission.

We as believers are on a mission for God. But tragedy has happened and we became separated by sin from God's purpose for our lives. Together we must now narrow our focus to safely getting home as we work together towards successfully entering the safe space of the kingdom while here on earth. We each are responsible for our part of the mission. When we discover what that personal mission is, we must write it down as a vision for our lives and ministry thus giving it our focus in order to maximize our influence and to accomplish the mission.

This is the reason why Higher Education starts with the level of Associate or Bachelor degrees, which includes a number of classes not necessarily relating to your field of interest. It is so you will develop your focus. Define your mission or career path. By the time you get to the PH.D level however you are now spending a ton of time focusing on one topic that you are specializing in. It is a matter of focus. The higher the level you want to achieve the narrower the focus becomes. You start by defining the mission, then narrower the focus becomes. To receive a Master's degree in Neurobiology one can spend years studying one specific nerve cell in one species of cricket. Now that is narrowing the focus; following one course until successful.

Allow me to offer a quick physics lesson as well. If you apply a certain amount of force to a large area, it will result in a certain amount of pressure. However, if you decrease the size of the area significantly, narrowing it, there will be a significant increase in pressure, even if the amount of force remains the same. What we are saying is this, if I hit your leg with a reasonable amount of force, you might say "Ouch." However, if I apply the same amount of force to a needle pointing directly to your leg, you will DEFINITELY scream from the pain. There will be a significantly greater impact because I focused on a significantly smaller or narrower area of your leg.

This same principle applies to how we spend our energy. Everyone has a certain amount of energy available on a daily basis. You can take that energy and apply it to a ton of different things and have a moderate affect, or you can focus all of your energy on a limited number of important things and have such a great impact that the world will "scream" from the affects of your focus. Having a narrowed focus allows you to cause as much damage as possible in the shortest amount of time, and I do mean that in a good way.

Many of us are stuck. At least we feel stuck. We feel powerlessly trapped doing things we could care less about, but feel like we have to or should do. When we do not reach our true goals or make an attempt, frustration and confusion sets in. "How do I break out of this cycle? Why can't I find the time to do the things that are important to me?" What we should be asking is, 'Why haven't I been making the time?' How can I narrow my focus?"

You and I have the same amount of time that Barack Obama, Martin Luther King Jr., Michael Jordan and Beyoncé had. Our usefulness of time depends on the choices we make and our focus. Unfortunately, it's to easy to make choices on the fly without a reference point – a grounded purpose or set of beliefs – to apply when making those decisions and choices. What you need is more focused time and focused points of reference. Focus Theology: helps us to see what God wants using reference points of focus which are" faith – obedience – commitment – unity and servant-hood. The way you live your life, from the career you choose all the way down to the way you pray, should fit within your values and beliefs, purpose and priorities.

With these priorities we focus to make better choices, and filter out the time-eaters that are actually optional. Do we really need to watch that much TV? Go to as many church conferences just to hear your favorite personality?

Hear as many approaches with no focus on having one of your own? Spend as much time on facebook or your cell phone talking to people about nothing? How many shoes and pairs of jeans can your wear at one time that makes shopping such a time eater?

The hard part is knowing the difference between what's important and what isn't. What's important are goals that support God's spiritual priorities and your focused approach to the roles you have as you live out and work through your God-given promises. What's not important are things that get in the way of your contribution to the purpose God has for you and the impact you can make for the kingdom.

In life, you can either be the hammer or the nail. You can apply force and energy where you want it to go, or you can react to the force and energy of others. The more you react instead of act, the harder it is to set your own direction. And the more likely it is that you'll wake up one day and wonder where you "went wrong?"

The first step to achieving goals "on purpose" is to define success and focus. You can go as far as creating a personal mission statement or just find a picture that presents your dreams clearly enough that it helps you to consciously follow. Even the shortest of short-term goals don't happen by accident. You have to purposefully decide what to do, where it fits in your day, and how to get it done.

Without direction and a map, you can get off course and end up in places you never wanted to go. Fifty things to do, many of which have nothing to do with your focus, can choke a typical day. When your mind and efforts are scattered like that, nothing gets done well, and some high priorities may get set aside or forgotten. With focus, distractions are kept to a minimum and your days are spent in a meaningful way. You regain control over your life, theology and approach to ministry and no longer feel like you're wasting time.

Focus helps you grab onto your goals with ferocity. Focus does not let go until the job is done. Focus is persistent, passionate, and stubborn. As you learn to live with passion, purpose and priorities, a motivating focus becomes even more important. Your focus will help you carry out your goals with passion, the right perspective and energy. Focusing gives you a solid foundation to work from. It's great to care about what you do, but you need to be moving in the right direction and that means you must focus.

People are naturally more motivated when they have a clear sense of purpose. Have you ever had an assignment that you couldn't see the purpose of? It may have been important to someone else, but certainly not to you. How motivated did you feel? How much did you look forward to doing that assignment? Chances are, not very much at all.

So how do you decide what to focus on?

Jesus lived and died under the old covenant. It was not until the resurrection and ascension that the foundations of the gospel were complete. Only then could the fullness of the gospel be preached. The last time I looked at the great commission that is exactly what Jesus told His disciples to preach.

In the last forty days Jesus was on earth he taught his disciples what was most important for them to know and teach. For forty days he focused them. He spoke about the kingdom of God, the coming of age of the Holy Spirit, and witnessing throughout the world (Acts 1:3-8). Things we focus on today like prosperity, parenting, marriage, and being happy did not make the curriculum of the forty day seminar on focus which was Jesus' last instructions while on earth.

Everything Jesus taught was true. But He focused on the teaching concerning the kingdom of heaven (Matthew 4:17). When He sent forth His disciples, He told them to focus on the message that the kingdom is at hand (Matthew. 10:7; Luke 10:11).

Jesus told his disciples that he had only introduced them to His message. The Holy Spirit was to come to finish the job and guide their focus. The Holy Spirit would guide the apostles into all truth (John 16:13). Therefore, what the apostles taught in sermon and epistle is as much the teaching of Jesus as the words that came directly from the lips of the Master.

Church growth gurus are telling us that our services are to be seeker oriented. Some are even saying that church services are not for Christians! They are designed for the "unchurched," that euphemistic concession to political correctness that we use nowadays to designate the lost, the left-out, and the left behind of the community not yet visited. So we employ music that the "unchurched" can gyrate to and praise choruses that are "gospelly" anemic and without godly focus in order to fill the pews. We use modern technology and every Madison Avenue strategy we can to market people into our churches and religious events and so-called Christian activities. When the truth is their focus is not on the kingdom of God but are strategies designed by and for this world. So from our praise and worship to the sermon itself does Godly focus become the priority for many in today's church? Even communion meditations often miss the mark in terms of explaining why we observe the sacraments of the church; that is if we observe them at all.

What then is the purpose of bringing the "unchurched" or the community not yet visited to church if they go home just entertained and not convicted, focused on the Savior or how they can turn their lives around and make an impact for the kingdom? What shall it profit a man (or woman) if they have an ideal marriage, raises outstanding children, has his or her finances in order, but lose their soul?

If the top three subjects we promote as addressing the gospel Jesus preached is marriage, parenting and finances then what do we do with the truth if the Scriptures that declare these were the least of Jesus' focus.

While reading about one scholar's focus on the red letter edition of the NIV version of the Bible, he points out what every red letter, or what Jesus said, in the four Gospels and what they were about. The writer classified each according to its primary teaching aim as indicated by context. This is no easy task. Some verses address more than one subject. For example, Jesus may refer to prayer and faith in a verse. Under what heading should we classify the verse? For statistical purposes they assigned one topic to each verse. Eliminated from the study were those few red letter verses where the disciples are merely repeating something Jesus said earlier. Here are some of the results you'll find.

In the four Gospels there are 1,854 red letter verses in which Jesus is directly speaking. Of these 341 are comments that clearly have no teaching value. For example, Jesus often engaged in casual conversation with His disciples or with those in His audience. Removing these non teaching verses left 1,513 verses to be studied for their context. Stay focused here!

The Gospel of Matthew had the most red letter teaching verses both in terms of raw numbers (1,071) and percentage (over 50%) of the total material in the book. The top subjects addressed in the teaching of Jesus were focused in this way:

(1) *Eternal life and salvation* (46 verses; 3, 04%);

(2) *Prayer* (48 verses; 3.17%);

(3) *Persecution* (54 verses; 3.57%;

(4) *Judgment and hell* (61 verses; 4.03%);

(5) *Predictions,* especially about His disciples and Himself (67 verses; 4:43%);

(6) *Hypocrisy* (73 verses; 4.82%);

(7) *Second coming* (79 verses; 5.22%);

(8) *Fate of Jerusalem and the evil generation that rejected Jesus* (119 verses; 7.87%);

(9) *Jesus' identity and mission* (129 verses; 8.53%). The subject that Jesus focused on the most however, was

(10) *The kingdom* (159 verses; 10.51%) - its nature, entrance, requirements and nearness. This was Jesus' primary focus.

For the record, you find 16 verses which had as their primary focus *marriage and divorce* (1.06%), and 43 verses (2.84%) that addressed *treasure and greed.* Frankly, you cannot find anything that Jesus said that had the primary focus of teaching about parenting. We can possibly count all the passages where Jesus referred to His heavenly Father and possibly use it as one whose topic could be classified as parenting. But truthfully we would be stretching the issue.

Why then do so many make the outlandish assertion that Jesus' focus was primarily on the subjects of marriage, parenting and finances? Even allowing for a difference of opinion on the classification of some of the verses, these subjects would not come close to representing the thrust of Jesus' focus. It seems to me that in the interest of sincere church spiritual development and personal growth as Christians, or ones whose focus is on following Christ, we are taking our cues more from Oprah and Dr. Phil rather than Jesus. As Dr. Phil likes to say, 'How is that working for you?"

Focus Theology is the opportunity to connect with a faith focus that reflects God's heart and intentions for us to make an impact for the kingdom. The focus is on projecting a ministry approach and life mission that develops and flourishes when: faith – obedience – commitment – unity – and servant-hood come together to support our theology and through prayers, resources, gifting and prioritizing of our time guides our approach to living out our Christian life and calling.

Focus Theology may include "hands-on" opportunities to participate in tangible support of a ministry or project. At other times, it helps as we focus on donating our time, treasure and talents toward ministry approaches that are needful for a broad base of support to accomplish a specific goal. Think about something you have tried to do that you just weren't good at. Maybe it was a sport, art, crafts, technical, cooking, math, musical instruction or cleaning up. God has made each of us with both strengths and weaknesses. We try something but sometimes we're just bad at it!

Somehow in ministry, we think it's different. We think we should all be great evangelists or good working with children or comfortable visiting sick people. Lord, help us with those who think pastoring is their call. But God has given each of us talents and gifts that prepare us for our own unique races. We must run our own race and quit trying to run someone else's. We must focus and follow that one course which God has for us to be successful.

Ever wonder why we sometimes feel like a failure, not realizing that we are not supposed to be good at everything? The Apostle Paul knew better. God called him to a particular race and that was his focus! The Christian race and mission involves our whole lives. We are all ministers. We all are to serve the kingdom and impact the world. Every part of our lives is part of the race – our jobs, our relationships, our leisure time. Everything is involved in God's plan for us to be his ambassadors to the world. It's not all about our service just to the church, although that is a big part of it. However, The Theology of Focus helps us to focus on that part of your race, mission, ministry and life within the body of Christ that helps you to make an impact in the world.

And since prayer is always essential for spiritual impact, our obedient commitment to unified prayer becomes the most important element of our faith focus as we follow one course until successful. Stay focused!

Jesus' Focus:

"I come: in the volume of the book it is written of me" (Psalm 40:7).

"The testimony of Jesus is the spirit of prophecy" (Revelation 19:10).

"...all things must be fulfilled, which were written in the law of Moses, and in the prophets, and in the psalms, concerning me" (Luke 24:44).

Defending the faith

Some people — even self-proclaimed Christians — today have one basic belief about the Bible — that it shouldn't be believed! But things didn't used to be that way. Prior to the late 20th century, virtually all people who claiming to be Christians understood Scripture to be inspired and preserved — in other words, sacred. Their belief was God had given His Word and they were to follow the Scriptures. The Bible is supposed to judge us, but some people would like to judge the Bible instead. Thus, in many ways this generation has lost its focus.

However, the Bible is trustworthy, and its trustworthiness begins with the core truth of inspiration: The Bible was written by God through men that we might focus on God and his purpose for our lives.

Many skeptics point out the Bible is not proven as God's Word just because some of its verses say so. Books like The Da Vinci Code, a Dan Brown novel, mix historical fact with fiction to confuse people about the authenticity of the Bible. The book raises a number of questions: "Is it true that man wrote the Bible hundreds of years after Jesus lived?" "Did people really fight over what the Bible was going to say?" "What if the things that ended up in the Bible weren't what God really meant the Bible to say?"

Christians have answers because the Bible's divine origin is supported by compelling evidence so there is unity to the Bible. The entire Bible was written by about 40 individuals over 1,500 years. These writers included a farmer (Amos), a doctor (Luke), ministers (such as Ezra and James), political leaders (David, Solomon), political prisoners (Daniel, John), a musician (Asaph), a fisherman (Peter) and a tax collector (Matthew).

Moses, who wrote the first five books of the Old Testament, grew up wealthy in Egypt, became a fugitive, herded livestock, then eventually led a nation. Paul, who wrote 13 books of the New Testament, was professionally trained in religion, theology and philosophy, and before he became a Christian led a movement to hunt down the followers of Jesus Christ. The Bible writers were rich and educated, poor and not-so-educated; they came from a wide variety of social backgrounds.

Yet the Bible contains a unified, consistent message of faith. It summarizes "God's Savior, and how you may know Him" or "The kingdom of heaven, and how to get in." The agreement woven throughout all 66 books written by different people at different times strongly points to the Bible's heavenly origin. Though humans did the writing, the Bible is the product of one author: God.

Churches and Christians didn't choose the books they wanted to put in the Bible. They eventually recognized the books that God had chosen. Bible expert J. I. Packer puts it this way: "The church no more "gave us" the canon than Sir Isaac Newton "gave us" the force of gravity. God gave us gravity by the work of His creation, and similarly, He gave us the New Testament canon by inspiring the original books that make it up."

Why Inspiration Matters

Because the Bible is God's Word and what it says was true when it was written, it is still true today and will be true tomorrow and forever. In the most crucial issues of life — like God, human nature, right and wrong, sin, forgiveness, death and eternity — you can't afford to guess what is true. Your life depends on whether what you believe is, in fact, true. It depends on your focus.

The origin, accuracy and relevancy of the Bible are important to each of us. Fortunately, the evidence strongly indicates that the Bible is indeed God's Word, preserved for us to read, understand and follow. Nearly 500 years ago, the great reformer Martin Luther gave us his take on God's Word: "In the Bible God speaks. The Scriptures are His word. To hear or read the Scriptures is nothing else than to hear God himself."

You could spend your entire life, as some scholars have, researching the evidence in support of the Bible's accuracy. However, as Luther said, if you want to hear the voice of God, open your Bible. A good, easy-to-understand starting point is the Gospel of John in the New Testament. You may want to pray the words of Psalm 119:18 as you begin to seriously study the Bible: "Open my eyes that I may see wonderful things in your law."

The Theology of Focus is about the Kingdom and establishing eternal perspective in us. Too many Christians focus on the temporal life in the flesh instead of maintaining an eternal perspective. Temporal – "relating to time as opposed to eternity" or of relating to earthly life rather than kingdom life.

The Kingdom of God is an eternal kingdom, an everlasting kingdom, and "Kingdom Focus" will establish us in the kingdom of God (now). Kingdom life will flow through you all of the time. You can live in kingdom atmosphere where God is ever-present. The word establishes the Kingdom of God, but it exists by power. It is manifest through power. The Kingdom of God that we live in is a kingdom of power.

It seems that this generation's focus has redefined what it means to be spiritual, and researchers are interested in discovering what this means for our society.

One graduate student researching the distinction youth make between spirituality and religion found that youth "define spirituality in terms of positive behaviors, feelings and relationships." Call it "Sensory Perception."

Although the assumption is that many people are 'spiritual,' spirituality is not something that is easy to articulate and define. People have a hard time separating spirituality from religion, but the differences are important to understanding behavior and development. Focus Theology is most interested in learning how spirituality affects positive development to make an impact in the world. But with the focus this generation now has on sensory perceptions what impact are we really making?

- Only 15 percent of emerging adults have a strong personal faith and practice it regularly.
- About 30 percent are engaged inconsistently or loosely affiliated with a religious tradition.
- One in four is indifferent toward religion, while 15 percent are open to spiritual or religious matters but haven't made a personal commitment.
- The final 15 percent have little or no connection to religion, or hold negative attitudes toward it.

Emerging adults tend to focus on church as sort of an elementary school for morals. Once we've got the basics of right and wrong, you eventually "graduate," perhaps returning when it's time for your own children to learn elementary morality.

This is a stark contrast to the idea of faith focus as a permanent, transcendent anchor of meaning amid crashing waves of change. Rather than the source of purpose being our purpose and faith focus, this generation seems to see a mere shadow of an important historical role for religious congregations: they see these congregations as providing community and support for individuals and families from womb to tomb but without any focus on God's approach as the primary focus and mission.

How do you define spirituality as distinct from religion? How can houses of worship help provide support for individuals throughout the stages of their lives? How can parents, adults and counselors help emerging adults find and develop their faith?

INTRODUCTION

PART B: Faith-Obedience-Commitment-Unity Servant-hood

Faith is a foundational principle in the scriptures. If we don't have faith, we don't have salvation. The Bible tells us that without faith, it is impossible to please God, therefore understanding faith is critical. If we don't understand faith then we will not understand our relationship with God nor can we mature spiritually. The Bible forewarned that when Jesus returns in the last days, He would not find genuine faith in the church. That does not mean He will not find individuals who have faith, but the church as a whole will be carried away with various doctrines that gratify human desires, offer primarily sensory perceptions and neglect the focus on true faith God has given us.

Confusion adds to this basic principle by those who claim to have 'faith formulas' that place the focus on self-gratification. Churches now teach that trials and troubles are the result of a lack of faith; sickness is a lack of faith; wealth and prosperity is the product of our own faith instead of the grace of God. The whole message of God's grace has always been the focus that it is a gift of God and not by anything we can merit so that no one can boast. However, under the 'new theology', today's spiritual leaders boast over their superior faith and condemn those who are going through a time of hardship for their lack of faith.

Those who sincerely seek the truth also struggle to make sense of it all because we analyze and over analyze faith until it becomes so complex that it cannot be understood. In error it has become a convoluted theological argument that cannot be grasped by the common man. Yet the Bible calls it a simple concept that even a child can understand; "Assuredly, I say to you, whoever does not receive the kingdom of God as a little child will by no means enter it" (Mark 10:15). Faith is so simple a child can focus and understand it, but so difficult to live by because our human nature gets in the way. Let's take a moment to examine what faith is.

What is faith?

Faith, simply, is believing God. Faith is not saying, "I believe God" or "I believe in God", but it is truly believing God. Look at Romans 4:3-5, "For what does the Scripture say?"Abraham believed God, and it was accounted to him for righteousness. Now to him who works, the wages are not counted as grace but as debt. But to him who does not work but believes on Him who justifies the ungodly, his faith is accounted for righteousness."

Obedience

2 Timothy 2:20-21 talks about being a vessel for honorable use. Paul says we are like the different kinds of dishes and pots in a large house: "Now in a great house there are not only vessels of gold and silver but also of wood and clay, some for honorable use, some for dishonorable. Therefore, if anyone cleanses himself from what is dishonorable, he will be a vessel for honorable use, set apart as holy, useful to the master of the house, ready for every good work." (2 Timothy 2:20-21)

Paul wants us to ask ourselves, which kind of vessel do I want to be in God's kingdom? If, as a Christian, I fill my mind and heart with the focus of "dishonorable" things before God, I can expect to be like a vessel for "dishonorable use" (like the scrub bucket or the garbage can or the dish we put the dog food in). God may still use me for something in his kingdom, but there won't be much blessing in it. But, if I turn away from things that dishonor God, if I keep from my eyes and my mind "what is dishonorable," then I will be to God like a dish made of gold or silver, "a vessel for honorable use ... ready for every good work." If we want God to use us in significant ways, we have to walk in obedience to him.

OBEDIENCE TO GOD

But Samuel replied: "Does the LORD delight in burnt offerings and sacrifices as much as in obeying the voice of the LORD? To obey is better than sacrifice, and to heed is better than the fat of rams. For rebellion is like the sin of divination, and arrogance like the evil of idolatry. Because you have rejected the word of the LORD, he has rejected you as king." (I Samuel 15:22, 23)

There are faith, hope, and love, and the greatest of these is love. But greater than love is obedience, if the love does not include obedience it is out of focus.

The greatest commandment is to love God with all our heart and strength. But implicit in that love is obedience. Genuine love for God works out in strict obedience to God. Apart from obedience to the Father there is no love for God and there is no Kingdom of God.

I am pointing out the obvious here because typical Christian thinking maintains that Christians are not required to obey God with a firm and focused commitment in view of the fact that we are "saved by grace."

I have a passion to do the perfect will of God. I hope I never lose it. I count it a great gift, one to be highly desired and sought after. However, the centrality of obedience to all that God has conceived has struck my mind and heart with renewed force.

When I began in ministry I was told that the world was waiting for someone to go all the way with God. I suppose what was meant was someone who would do God's perfect will. So passionately with this focus I volunteered. I told the Lord that if He would give me the opportunity and provide the ability I would do whatever He desired—no matter what. Then I did not know what to expect, so great was my ignorance.

About that time I was called to come to California and I told the Lord I would go wherever He indicated. I have discovered something since that time. I know now that nothing else is acceptable to God but obedience. He expects every person to do His perfect will from the heart. Instead of being some extraordinary consecration, doing God's perfect will from the heart is the only acceptable attitude. One cannot have fellowship with God apart from this.

The King James version of the Bible suggests, in Romans 12:1, 2, that there are three wills of God: an acceptable will, a good will, and a perfect will. "I beseech you therefore, brethren, by the mercies of God, that ye present your bodies a living sacrifice, holy, acceptable unto God, which is your reasonable service. And be not conformed to this world: but be ye transformed by the renewing of your mind, that ye may prove what is that good, and acceptable, and perfect, will of God." (Romans 12:1, 2)

But note the New International version: "Therefore, I urge you, brothers, in view of God's mercy, to offer your bodies as living sacrifices, holy and pleasing to God—this is your spiritual act of worship. Do not conform any longer to the pattern of this world, but be transformed by the renewing of your mind. Then you will be able to test and approve what God's will is—his good, pleasing and perfect will." (Romans 12:1, 2)

There is only one will of God, and it is good, pleasing, and perfect. It is not at all true that there are three wills of God. There is only the one will of God for us to focus on at any given time, obviously. How could it be otherwise? Either we are doing God's will or we are not doing God's will! The problem in God's creation is that of rebellion against His will. Apparently Satan was the first rebel, and from Satan has spread the virus of disobedience. Adam and Eve disobeyed God. All other sins spring from the one sin of disobedience.

Satan filtered into Christian consciousness the concept that no one can do God's will; and so we must be saved by "grace." By this is meant God recognizes we cannot do His will and so He pardons us if we will "accept Christ." This is a monumental error, on two counts.

First, God's perfect will for any person at any given time is always practical and possible. His commandments are not grievous. Whereas one can never please Satan, God is relatively easy to please in most instances when we focus on pleasing Him.

Second, receiving Christ never is an alternative to doing God's will. Rather, receiving Christ is the beginning of the program of redemptive focus that leads us to the place where we always do God's will from the heart. Would the new covenant be a better covenant if its end result was people who still were disobedient to God? What foolishness and ignorance pass for Divine truth in our day!

No temptation has taken us except that which is common to man. God always makes a way of escape so we may be able to bear it. The idea that no person can do

God's perfect will is a lie—a lie calculated to keep God's people from drawing close to Him. The perfect will of God is not perfection but perfectly obedient and committed to being focused on His will for our lives.

My next statement is radical in the true sense of the word. If I am correct, we Christians need to refocus what we are teaching. The fundamental concept of Christian teaching is false. The fundamental concept is that the purpose of salvation is to enable people when they die to avoid Hell and enter Paradise. This concept is not scriptural. It comes from a humanistic view of the Gospel. It is man-centered, not God-centered. It says nothing about solving God's problem of rebellion against His will. It brings man to Paradise without solving God's problem.

The purpose of salvation is not to bring rebels to Paradise, believers who never have been saved from worldliness, the lusts of the flesh, or their self-will.

The purpose of salvation is to bring Christ into the human personality to form a new creation. The new creation is an indissoluble blend of Christ and the individual.

The new creation always obeys God strictly, in every detail. Divine grace, properly understood and applied, does not bring rebellious people into Paradise. Divine grace converts the rebellious until they are obedient. While this may appear to be such a truism that it need not be considered carefully, current Christian teaching and procedures proclaim forgiveness and largely ignore the critical need for actual conversion of character.

"Ah," one may exclaim, "the prostitutes, thieves and the addicted enter the Kingdom readily, going in advance of the religious even", true enough. The reason is, the prostitutes addicts and thieves repent and change their ways until they are obeying God, whereas the religious trust in the beliefs and practices of their religion while their hearts remain far from God. When God decided to answer the rebellion of Satan He conceived a great plan. He would take the WORD, test Him to the limit, and when proven in obedience He would make Him a great Vine from which branches would grow and also be proven in obedience. Then the Vine and the branches would serve as judges of angels and of the peoples of the world.

So the Word was made flesh. He was tested in every conceivable manner. Finally He was presented with the decision to risk His eternal destiny; His fellowship was with the Father, in order to bear the sins of the world on Himself. He united in faith with those who in obedience would become His servants, committed to the kingdom He brought with Him.

This He did, in an agony of doubt and oppression. The Son of God emerged in triumph, having obeyed His Father to the last breath. Because of His obedience, which He learned while on the earth, He has been given all authority in Heaven, upon the earth, and over all the inhabitants of the dark dungeons under the earth's surface.

This is the beginning of God's answer to the rebellion of Satan, although the offering of Isaac was a forerunner of the answer, making the obedient Abraham the father of all who believe. The obedient Vine has been planted in God. Now there are to be obedient branches growing out from the Vine.

Jesus said if we did not bear fruit we would be removed from the Vine. Why is this? It is because the fruit is the moral image of Christ. The most important element of the fruit is strict obedience to God, the keeping of His commandments.

If we receive Christ and then are not obedient to God, we are not fulfilling God's purpose in grafting us on the Vine. We then shall be removed from the Vine because we are not solving God's problem.

Some are teaching that we can be cut out of the Vine but we will still be "saved," meaning we will go to Heaven when we die. This is how entrenched the Christian myth is. It does not matter whether or not we remain in the Vine, in Christ, just as long as we go to our mansion in Heaven. It does not matter whether God is pleased or served, just as long as we escape Hell and go to Heaven.

It absolutely is true that we can be saved from wrath by believing in Christ and being baptized in water. But until we begin to obey God we are part of the problem of rebellion in God's creation. No believer who has not learned to obey God in all matters will ride behind Christ in the Day of the Lord. No believer who has not learned to obey God in all matters will be a part of the New Jerusalem, the glorified Christian Church.

All the promises we associate with being a Christian will be fulfilled in the victorious saints, that is, in those who have learned to obey God in any and all situations. Think about the following statement. Is it true? Christian theology really is a device to get people into Paradise without ever having to learn to obey God. Thus it is destructive of the Divine program and is in my opinion out of focus.

But Samuel replied: "Does the LORD delight in burnt offerings and sacrifices as much as in obeying the voice of the LORD? To obey is better than sacrifice, and to heed is better than the fat of rams. For rebellion is like the sin of divination, and arrogance like the evil of idolatry. Because you have rejected the word of the LORD, he has rejected you as king." (I Samuel 15:22, 23)

To obey the voice of the Lord is better than all religious practices—all religious practices! The Lord is more delighted with someone who obeys Him than with hundreds of people who are pursuing their religious activities. We must start off as a Christian by studying the scriptures and asking the Holy Spirit to help us obey the numerous commandments and focus our commitment to on the principles they offer therein. Some are not even doing this nowadays. As we mature in the Lord we become conscious of His will for our life. As we present our body a living sacrifice we are able to prove the will of God. Eventually we find ourselves looking to the Lord for every decision we make.

However, a multitude of the members of the Christian religion have no such sense of the Lord's will. And when they think God wants them to do something they are as likely to disobey as they are to obey. They trust they are saved by some mysterious force termed "grace" and so they proceed on their merry way.

They simply do not understand to not be obeying God is to not be a Christian at all, only a member of the "Christian religion." "Rebellion is like the sin of divination, and arrogance like the evil of idolatry." These words were spoken to King Saul who did not obey God in the matter of the Amalekites (I Samuel 15:23).

Saul attacked and defeated them, but then he added some modifications of his own. He was not like Moses who did precisely what the Lord commanded—in every detail. Why is rebellion like the sin of divination? Divination is a way of accomplishing one's goals apart from the will of God.

Why is arrogance like the evil of idolatry? Again, idolatry is the worship of a god and obedience to that god instead of to the Lord. In the case of arrogance, it is the worship of one's self. The "just shall live by faith" means the righteous individual lives by strict obedience and focus on the Lord instead of by his or her own talents and desires.

What does it take to learn obedience to the Lord? First, we must deny ourselves. We must decide once and for all that we are the Lord's servant and will do whatever He wishes. Until we get down before God and tell Him we are His servants and will do whatever He wishes, we have not started on the Christian discipleship journey. Thus most Christian believers are not disciples. They are happy religious people, but they are not true Christian disciples.

But will they be "saved" and go to Heaven anyway? That is the important question of focused theology. There is no love for God here, no true repentance, just membership in a religion.

We must take up our cross. Our cross is that painful, frustrating circumstance that we cannot get rid of without breaking God's laws. There is a multitude of Christians today who would never consent to go year after year in painful, frustrating circumstances. They say, "God wants me to be happy." Then they proceed to forsake their husband or wife, their children, their church and their God.

After we deny ourselves and are willing to carry our cross—to the end of our days if need be—we must follow the Master. The Lord Jesus wants us to talk to Him continually. Every aspect of our day and night is held before the Lord. This may sound difficult, but it quickly becomes as natural as breathing.

There is no true Christian life other than denying ourselves, taking up our cross, and following Jesus. All the rest is the contrived focus of "Christian religion." We learn obedience to God by denying ourselves, taking up our cross, and following the Lord Jesus.

Commitment

God also promises Abraham that he would be the father of many nations and through his seed all the nations of the earth would be blessed. Later, God promised that Abraham would father a son in his old age and that through his son Isaac the promise would be fulfilled. God then calls Abraham to action. Before Isaac was born, God said, "Sarah your wife shall bear you a son, and you shall call his name Isaac; I will establish my covenant with him for an everlasting covenant, and with his descendants after him."

Afterward, when Isaac was still a youth, God put Abraham's faith to the test as revealed in Genesis 22:2-5, "Then He said, "Take now your son, your only son Isaac, whom you love, and go to the land of Moriah, and offer him there as a burnt offering on one of the mountains of which I shall tell you. So Abraham rose early in the morning and saddled his donkey, and took two of his young men with him, and Isaac his son; and he split the wood for the burnt offering, and arose and went to the place of which God had told him. Then on the third day Abraham lifted his eyes and saw the place afar off. And Abraham said to his young men, "Stay here with the donkey; the lad and I will go yonder and worship, and we will come back to you."

There are two very important points in this passage that reveal true faith in God. First, Abraham demonstrated faith because he did not delay (he was obedient). He rose up early in the morning and headed out. God did not have to keep pressing Abraham for obedience; he obeyed immediately.

The second important thing to note is Abraham's testimony in verse 5 of his belief in God's promise, "the lad and I will go...and we will come back". God clearly promised that Isaac would be the heir and through him God would establish the covenant and His promise to Abraham. (Commitment)

Commitment is following Jesus. "Commitment demands a choice." Jesus wasted no time getting to the heart of commitment: Either the disciples would be committed to Him and deny their own desires. Or they would be determined to go their own ways and deny Him. The choice to commit is the same for all believers - either deny ourselves or deny Him; either we follow His way or we pursue our own way.

Talk about Christ would be meaningless without the walk with Him. The disciples were to take up their crosses. Carrying the cross beam was a public declaration of Rome's authority. Jesus challenged them to put themselves voluntarily under God's authority, doing His will His way. Commitment demands action; it cannot be divorced from responsibility. It extends beyond our relationship to the heavenly Father to other areas of life.

Ruth's words of commitment to Naomi did not speak as loudly as did her actions. She left her family and homeland to return with Naomi to Bethlehem. Commitment definitely limits choices because it is exclusive. For example, in a commitment to marriage, God's plan is for one woman and one man to commit to each other exclusively and permanently.

Commitment builds up faith and develops character. It is a spiritual discipline requiring time, work and determination." Commit comes from the Latin word which means to bind together. When I think of commitment I think of a rope and Ecclesiastes 4:12 which says in part, "a threefold cord is not quickly broken." Faith, obedience and commitment form a cord that is not easily broken.

Calling is the truth that God calls us to Himself so decisively that everything we are, everything that we do, and everything we have is an investment with a special devotion, dynamism and direction lived out as a response to His summons and service.

Several words are utilized to express commitment. First, commitment communicates the entrusting of something valuable to another person [Gk tithemi— to commit, commend, assign; paradidomi— to give over, commit]. Second, commitment additionally includes the responsibility to practice specific activities [Gk poieo— to do, cause, commit; prasso— to do, practice, commit].

God entrusts or commits a valuable deposit unto each believer that is to be guarded and protected, that is to be faithfully proclaimed, followed, or exercised, and in turn is to be committed to others. Each believer is responsible to respond to God's call by committing their heart, mind, body, and life to serve Him, to share the Gospel, and to be His ambassadors in this world.

Our life is a testimony of faith or unbelief. Obedience and commitment! When we withhold any area of our life from God, we will never find the provision God has already prepared for us. God never reveals the end result until we have already stepped out in faith become obedient and make a commitment to do it God's way. True faith is believing God and acting upon it.

Look at Hebrews 11:1, "Now faith is the substance of things hoped for, the evidence of things not seen." The word substance has caused confusion because some take this out of context and make it mean that faith is a force and something we possess or harness. There are two words translated into the word substance in scripture.

One comes from the Greek word, huparchonta {hoop-ar'-khon-tah}. This word means possessions. In this passage in Hebrews, the word used is hupostasis {hoop-os'-tas-is}, which means foundation, confidence, assurance, or a firm trust. True faith is absolute confidence in God. It is believing God so firmly that His promises are all the evidence needed.

We know that even if we have to sacrifice the things that are precious to us, God will not only restore all that is lost, but will do so abundantly above anything we can expect. It is also knowing with firm assurance that the greater promise is eternal and will not pass away.

Our faith is not something we produce, but it is believing God so firmly that we are willing to go wherever God commands or endure whatever God requires. Jesus taught that faith is in God, not in faith and not my ability to produce faith. If I am the focus, it is not true faith. 1 John 5:4-5 says, "For whatever is born of God overcomes the world. And this is the victory that has overcome the world -- our faith. Who is he who overcomes the world, but he who believes that Jesus is the Son of God?"

We rise above trials and overcome this world by our faith and our faith believes in Jesus Christ. This is the Focused Theology. We follow Christ with firm assurance that He is who the Bible says He is and will do what He has promised to do. Nothing this world can throw at us will uproot us from our foundation in the Rock of Jesus Christ.

The Unity of the Faith

The unity of the faith is a centerpiece concept in the New Testament. Christ, our Lord, prayed for it just before his crucifixion in John 17:20-21: "My prayer is not for them alone. I pray also for those who will believe in me through their message, that all of them may be one, Father, just as you are in me and I am in you. May they also be in us so that the world may believe that you have sent me."

The apostle Paul wrote vividly about this same unity of faith in Ephesians 4:12-13, ". . . that the body of Christ may be built up until we all reach unity in the faith and in the knowledge of the Son of God and become mature, attaining to the whole measure of the fullness of Christ." All Christians must strive for unity of the faith to build up the body of Christ.

The Bible Condemns Division

The Bible condemns the opposite of unity—division—in Galatians 5: 19-21, where we find that those who practice such things will not inherit the kingdom of God: "The acts of the sinful nature are obvious: sexual immorality, impurity and debauchery; idolatry and witchcraft; hatred, discord, jealousy, fits of rage, selfish ambition, dissensions, factions and envy; drunkenness, orgies, and the like. I warn you, as I did before, that those who live like this will not inherit the kingdom of God."

The largest group of the acts of a sinful nature is divisive sins: hatred, discord, and jealousy, fits of rage, selfish ambition, dissensions, factions and envy. Notice that those who practice such things will not inherit the kingdom of God. The church cannot be strong when the members participate in these sinful acts.

In 1 Corinthians 1:10-13, Paul condemns division in the strongest terms: "I appeal to you, brothers, in the name of our Lord Jesus Christ, that all of you agree with one another so that there may be no divisions among you and that you may be perfectly united in mind and thought. My brothers, some from Chloe's household have informed me that there are quarrels among you. What I mean is this: One of you says, "I follow Paul"; another, "I follow Apollos"; another, "I follow Cephas"; still another, "I follow Christ. Is Christ divided?"

What Paul confronted in Corinth is not unlike the divisions that exist in the 21st century church. False Teaching Interferes with Building up the Church. The New Testament teaches clearly that our job is to work toward unity and keep division away from this congregation. However, when confronted with divisive deeds or false teaching, the New Testament instructs us to take decisive and clear action. Paul tells us, in Romans 16:17-18, to watch out and keep away from those who cause division: "I urge you, brothers, to watch out for those who cause divisions and put obstacles in your way that are contrary to the teaching you have learned. Keep away from them. For such people are not serving our Lord Christ, but their own appetites. By smooth talk and flattery, they deceive the minds of naive people."

Paul admonishes elders in Titus 1:9-11 of the particular responsibility for protecting the congregation from divisive false teachers: "He must hold firmly to the trustworthy message as it has been taught, so that he can encourage others by sound doctrine and refute those who oppose it. There are many rebellious people, mere talkers and deceivers, especially those of the circumcision group. They must be silenced, because they are ruining whole households by teaching things they ought not to teach — and that for the sake of dishonest gain."

We must work to attain the unity of the faith, to protect that unity once we attain it, and to refute those who contradict the sound doctrine that supports it. The elders, as shepherds of the flock, must take the lead in achieving the unity of the faith. To this end, they need your help and prayers." Gossip and backbiting interfere with building up the Church.

Some aim the divisive acts of a sinful nature in Galatians 5 at fellow church members-- hatred, discord, jealousy. These sinful acts hurt the individual Christians at whom they are aimed and the entire local congregation. We cannot attain the unity of the faith and build up the congregation when members practice such sins.

In 2 Corinthians 12:20-21, Paul summarized the acts that are so destructive to the congregation: "I fear that there may be quarreling, jealousy, outbursts of anger, factions, slander, gossip, arrogance and disorder." Once one throws slander and gossip out on the gossip network, it is gone forever. One can never retrieve a lying message. Such gossip is as if a person tears open a feather pillow, throws the feathers to the wind, and then tries in desperation to retrieve the feathers. The feather—and the gossip—are gone forever.

The Divine Recipe for Unity and Building up the Church

God has given the church a recipe for attaining and maintaining the unity of the faith in the local congregations. Philippians 2:1-5, describes how we may be united in Christ: "If you have any encouragement from being united with Christ, if any comfort from his love, if any fellowship with the Spirit, if any tenderness and compassion, then make my joy complete by being like-minded, having the same love, being one in spirit and purpose. Do nothing out of selfish ambition or vain conceit, but in humility consider others better than yourselves. Each of you should look not only to your own interests, but also to the interests of others. Your attitude should be the same as that of Christ Jesus: We should be like-minded with the mind of Christ."

Let us pray that at the end of our time, the congregation where we attend will still be a faithful, unified, true and sincerely focused church of the Lord. We can only achieve this goal if we continually seek to build up the body of Christ till we attain the unity of the faith. Ephesians 4:12-13 bears repeating:, ". . . that the body of Christ may be built up until we all reach unity in the faith and in the knowledge of the Son of God and become mature, attaining to the whole measure of the fullness of Christ."

Servant-hood - Living by Faith

Look at these two passages from Hebrews: Hebrews 10:38-39, "Now the just shall live by faith; But if anyone draws back, my soul has no pleasure in him. But we are not of those who draw back to perdition, but of those who believe to the saving of the soul." Hebrews 11:6, "But without faith it is impossible to please Him, for he who comes to God must believe that He is, and that He is a rewarder of those who diligently seek Him."

There are many who begin in faith because they focus on the promise, but withdraw because of the sacrifices that God requires. God will test your faith and He will ask you to give up anything that is more important than God or anything that you trust in more than God. Jesus said in Luke 9:23-24, "Then He said to them all, If anyone desires to come after Me, let him deny himself, and take up his cross daily, and follow Me. For whoever desires to save his life will lose it, but whoever loses his life for My sake will save it."

This is a hard saying and very few will answer the call to follow Christ. No one can lay down their life, take up their cross daily and follow Him – unless they understand and apply their hearts to faith in God. Until we live by faith, it is impossible to please God. Until we truly believe that God is who He has revealed Himself to be and truly believe that He is the rewarder who fulfills His promises, we will never be willing to make that sacrifice. God calls us to focus and step into the unknown. God calls us to lay down our lives. God calls us to pick up the burden of the cross. God calls us to lay down anything that we value more than obedience to Him and offer ourselves as living sacrifices holy and acceptable to Him as our reasonable service (Romans 12:1).

In return, He has promised to perfect us, justify us, establish us and reward us abundantly above all that we could think or ask. We must first step out in faith and then God will take us by the hand and guide us through focused faith. You then stand at the crossroads: do you value and believe God's promises, or do you value your life in this world? At this moment of decision, most will draw back.

Before we move on, let's clarify another common problem with the concept of living by faith as God's servants. Many people fall into the trap of thinking that faith means denying reality. Contrary to common opinion, faith is not the absence of doubt, but trusting God in spite of our fears. Doubt and fear are an undeniable part of our human nature. Fear and doubt are of the flesh, but faith is a spiritual attribute. Our flesh and our spirit in Christ are at war against each other (Galatians 5). The Bible tells us that God has dealt each person a measure of faith. The Bible also states that we can see God work with only a mustard seed of faith. In other words, God has given us everything we need to focus and begin our walk of faith. God does not demand perfection – God works within us to produce perfection. The work is from God, not from us.

When God brings us to the point of decision, our human nature will be fearful and doubtful. It is important to understand this for a couple of reasons. First, if we think that we can only act once we have rooted out all doubt, it will be very rare that we will have the confidence to act. Second, it is unhealthy to pretend that real fears and doubts do not exist. When we pretend that we don't have doubts we are trying to fool God into doing what we think He should do. God knows our feelings and nothing is gained by trying to trick God or trick ourselves into thinking we have no concerns.

Faith in God is real. We don't need to play make-believe and act like nothing is wrong. God expects honesty, not pretense. When we live in denial, we are trying to use our own strength to accomplish the thing that only God can accomplish. God increases our faith – we do not. Our obedience plays a vital role in God's work in our life, but He is still the One who authors and finishes our faith. He deals us a measure of faith (enough to obey) and then works in our lives to fulfill His work. Our only role is to submit or resist the will of God. We must make a commitment.

It is disturbing to see someone suffering physically and 'claim their healing' by denying that the symptoms exist. I have seen people dying of cancer while saying, "I refuse to acknowledge this because God has healed me". When people die and their family is in denial, is faith increased or overthrown? They are now required to continue in self-deception and they must find an excuse for their loved one's death.

We see example after example in scripture of great men of faith who acknowledge their doubts. Abraham believed God but in Genesis 15 he asked God how is this promise to be fulfilled seeing he was old and had no son? While journeying by God's direction, Abraham was afraid that the Egyptians would kill him for his wife, so he told them Sarah was his sister.

Gideon obeyed God in spite of his fear. The story of Gideon is found in Judges Chapters 6 and 7. God spoke to Gideon and commanded him to destroy the idols in the land and then prepare to defeat the Midian army that held Israel in bondage. The Midianites had a mighty army that was described as numerous as sand on the seashore. God called Gideon to reduce his army to 300 men. Even though Gideon knew the will of God and was acting in obedience, he was afraid and had doubts. He asked God for a sign to verify that God was with him. He put a fleece out and asked God to show that if He was really going to give him this victory, let there be dew on the ground but not on the fleece. The next morning he saw that the ground was wet and the fleece was dry. He was still doubtful and the next night he asked God to let the fleece be wet and the ground dry.

Gideon knew the will of God; he heard the voice of God; God miraculously raised Gideon from a lowly farmer's son who was unknown to Israel to the leader of Israel's army. Events and circumstances clearly reveal the will of God and Gideon's call in that plan, yet he was unfocused still struggling with doubt. God called Gideon to use 300 men to defeat a powerful army numbering in the tens of thousand or possibly hundreds of thousand of soldiers. He was afraid and did not know how God would do this, yet he steps out in faith, obeys God and turns from fear to focus his faith and make a commitment to unit with God's promise and serve him even if what was being asked seemed so unrealistic. As a result of following one course until successful Gideon is listed in the 'faith hall of fame' that is found in Hebrews 11. Gideon had doubts, but the Bible calls him a great man of faith.

Moses is considered one of the greatest men of faith in scripture, yet when God first called him, he insisted on his brother Aaron being his spokesman. When he went before Pharaoh, he would talk to Aaron and Aaron would then talk to Pharaoh on Moses' behalf. In time, Moses became confident and boldly spoke to Pharaoh and became a strong leader over Israel. God used an insecure, fearful Moses to lead Israel out of bondage, to deliver the law to Israel and to write the first 5 books of the Old Testament. Faith calls us often to unite and share our faith with others as we serve and obediently make a commitment to God's purpose and plan.

Nehemiah was burdened because Jerusalem was in ruins and the people were violating God's law. He prayed and fasted for the opportunity to ask Artaxerxes, king of Persia, to allow him to go and rebuild Jerusalem. When the opportunity came, Nehemiah said, "I became dreadfully afraid". In spite of his fears, he followed God and was used by God to become a restorer of Israel – both by repairing the city and building up the spiritual lives of the people.

Elijah was one of the mightiest prophets in the Old Testament, but when Jezebel threatens him, he was afraid, ran for his life and begged God to take his life. The apostle Peter was afraid of the leaders of Israel and three times denying that he ever knew Jesus. All of these men and many others were used mightily by God in spite of their fears. Yet they became obedient through their commitment to focus and unit with God's purpose as His servant.

God did not demand fearless faith; God showed His power and built their faith. God used weak men who making an obedient commitment to unit with Him and others as his servant were able to accomplish mighty works. The only strength in their lives was the Solid Rock of God's power. Faith focus does not mean that you hide your fears; faith is believing and obeying God in spite of doubts and in spite of fears.

The Theology of Focus is believing in God and becoming obedient, making a lasting commitment to unite in faith and fidelity to impact the world as servants of the kingdom on a mission.

FOCUS

Enjoying the Grace; Extending the Glory; Establishing the Throne

From the laying on of hands to the casting out of demons the bible is full of examples that offer us a look at the effective use of power and authority. The season of consecration calls the church to focus on her access to heaven through Jesus Christ as her High Priest that we might enjoy the grace, extend the glory and establish the throne of the kingdom of God. As the church FOCUSES: her faith, obedience, commitment, unity and servant-hood she draws near to God; enjoying the Grace; extending the Glory; establishing the Throne of Christ and His kingdom on earth.

This dimension of kingdom life is not for those, who like lone rangers attempt to work their specialized ministries without bridging their FOCUS (faith, obedience, commitment, unity and servant-hood) in cooperation with the purpose of the church. Resisting evil is a key component of the gospel ministry given to the every believer in the church to practice within it and beyond it reaching the uttermost parts of the earth. Believers literally make up the Body of Christ on earth, and carry the seed of His life through the indwelling of His Spirit. However, when God the Father raised Jesus from the dead and returned Him to heaven, the enemy no longer had access to afflict Him as the seed of redemption.

Following Jesus' baptism, the bible says, the Spirit of God took Him into the wilderness of Judea. There Satan made his move immediately to tempt Jesus and God in His sovereignty allowed it as a test to prove the superior power and authority of His Son. When Jesus emerged victoriously, He immediately proclaimed the power and authority of the kingdom of God with signs and wonders. One of the signs was the exposure and expulsion of evil spirits; prophetically proclaimed in Genesis 3:15; "He will crush the enemies head." What the church lacks in its focus about the text is that it goes on to say, "and the enemy will strike his heel." This is spiritual warfare and as New Testament believers we are in an ongoing attempt by the evil one to destroy the seed of the life of God's chosen redeemer Jesus Christ, the Lord. Jesus claimed victory over the evil one as He crushed the power of Satan and took authority in the wilderness, in the Garden of Gethsemane and finally on the Cross. Having reclaimed all power and authority in heaven and on earth He returned to heaven and reclaimed His throne.

The forces of darkness, in their unrelenting attempt to destroy the seed, will continue to try and bruise Christ's Body until they are judged and bound when Jesus returns. Christians are born again according to I Peter 1:23; born again with the very life of Christ, the imperishable seed the bible says. But the church will continue to take hits of spiritual attacks, abuse and accusations from the evil one. In reaction, we are to engage our FOCUS (faith, obedience, commitment, unity and servant-hood) to overcome the schemes of the devil's warfare against us.

In Romans 16:20, Paul closes his correspondence to the Church at Rome by saying, "The God of peace will soon crush Satan under your feet." Notice that it is God doing the crushing, but it is our feet doing the victory dance on the devil's head. In Jesus Christ, complete victory over the evil one has been accomplished. We as believers, making up local congregations, have the responsibility to receive the power and authority as provision and protection; putting the powers of darkness in their place. The concern of most believers is with the daily struggles they face in life; instead of focusing on the greater cosmic issues of the spiritual warfare being waged on the Body of Christ. It is this daily life that is the target of the enemy and this is where we face issues relating to our own spiritual survival, protection of our children and finding God's power to deal with the trials and bondages we face.

The question is how do we receive the protection from the evil one promised by Jesus? How do we deal with our friends and loved ones caught up in the snare of drug addiction? What do we offer as protection for disintegrating marriages or the negative diseases of infidelity, lack of integrity, and lost sense of responsibility of those who lead in the home, community and the church? How do we pray for our children attacked by the temptations of the enemy daily as they go to and from school and back home again? What must we do to protect our youth and ourselves from the predatory stranger, who like a roaring lion is seeking to kill, steal and destroy lives through negative television programming, the Internet, on the street, at the mall, on our cell phones, through our unfocused conversations, abuses in our homes and destructive activities in our neighborhoods and unfaithful actions in the church?

My question is does your focus provide power and authority to deal with the spiritual warfare being waged against you? We have confused the need for the presence of God with the need for the power found in the authority of the glory of God. Psalm 97:10-11 says, "Let those who love the LORD hate evil, for he guards the lives of his faithful ones and delivers them from the hand of the wicked. Light shines on the righteous and joy on the upright of heart."

People confuse power with authority and they are not the same. As authority increases in the church power will increase. The truth of the matter is that no demon can stand to be in the presence of Godly authority. Yet, demons can operate around the use of power. We want power when what we need is authority. Godly authority only comes from an authentic relationship with God. Gifting and authority are also confused by those in the Body of Christ. Power is a gift that is given. We don't deserve it and it has nothing to do with anything that we have done. However, it is different from authority, which comes exclusively by relationship. Through your authentic relationship with God the authority of heaven is bestowed upon you. It is the fruit of a relationship with heaven.

Though each of us are given a measure of power and authority at salvation most of us usually focus on power and relinquish authority through the authentic pursuit of a sincere relationship with God. We want the power to do rather than the authority to use it. The devil, called Lucifer, was created with certain powers and authority. He was given authority by his close proximity to God. As a result of being removed from the presence of God, when Jesus said," I saw Satan fall from heaven like lightning"; at that moment Satan lost his authority but kept his power. The gifts and callings of God are without repentance. Therefore the power Satan has is irrevocable once God gives it. That is why so many people have power, great gifting and are wonderfully talented in areas of ministry and performance. Though they have the gift of power, they lack the authority through an authentic relationship with heaven to use it effectively or victoriously for God's glory. Like Lucifer, we choose power over authority and lose it through rebellion and lack of focus according to Ezekiel 28 "Lucifer was an anointed cherub who covers; I have established you; you were on the holy mountain of God." This indicates high office of authority and responsibility to protect and defend the mountain of God, or God's established throne.

Satan was a ruler over various sanctuaries - the bible says in Ezekiel 28:18; in heaven he was a worship leader until iniquity severed the relationship he had with God. This high place of authority afforded Satan (here named Lucifer) the unique opportunity to bring glory to God (v.13). But though he continued to have power he lost his authority as he attempted to seek glory for himself (Isaiah 14:12-17).

When the Archangel Michael was contending for the body of Moses with Satan it is a picture of power against power according to Jude 1:9 NLT. "But even Michael, one of the mightiest of the angels, did not dare accuse the devil of blasphemy, but simply said, "The Lord rebuke you!" (This took place when Michael was arguing with the devil about Moses' body.). So he used their authority to invoke the name of the Lord as he said, "the lord rebukes you." Then using the authority of heaven he could take control of Moses body from the enemy. Michael did not use his authority as an archangel against the authority of Lucifer, who was also an Archangel instead he used the authority of the name of the most high.

Likewise, character then is also a fruit of the authentic relationship with God. One cannot spend time around he who is holy and not become holy. Righteousness is the outgrowth of our relationship with God towards others, while holiness is our relationship with God. Righteousness and holiness combined create a character that is truly godly in its outgrowth to other people; allowing God to trust us so that we will not misuse the authority he places on us.

Again, it is important to note that we all have God given gifts. The gifts of the Holy Spirit dwelling in us we have access to. Yet, without the proper focus we need to have regarding our authority results in much of the chaotic circumstances we see in our leadership or lack thereof in the church today. When people don't walk under authority they don't have authority.

The Centurion soldier remarks to Jesus saying "will you go and heal my servant?" Jesus said, "I will go." But the Centurion being under authority himself, said you don't even have to go." I see the authority you are operating under and all you have to do is say the word. This is what made demons so terribly uncomfortable and Jesus did not have to even say a word when confronting them. The authority he carried in his authentic relationship with heaven was evident to them and they immediately came under authority though they themselves had power from Satan.

The woman with the issue of blood understood this authority as well when she merely uttered, "if I can but touch the hem of the Lord's garment, I will be healed." The year of fulfilled promises is the Lord's desire for us to walk in his authority again and to enjoy the grace, extend the glory, and establish the throne. Especially as we encounter these last and difficult days as His body. To do this we must understand there is nothing wrong with having power for it is a truly wonderful gift from God. But only through our intimate and personal relationship with Christ are we provided authority.

This power is the word "dunamis" the root word for dynamite or dynamic ministry. This is the empowered church, explosive in nature and provides creative change and nurture. But "exousia" is the word for 'authority" which is the ability to rule after you've conquered the ability to change things.

When Jesus said, "the Spirit of the Lord is upon me, to heal the brokenhearted, to set the captives free, to release those imprisoned, etc.", HE was saying God has given me authority. Then he said, "to preach the acceptable year of the LORD." In other words, the time when God's authority will be made manifest and this has been fulfilled in your sight. The promises of God are about to be released right in front of you. The people marveled at his power and authority. What people are amazed about far too often today is the use and often misuse of power and forget the need for having the authority to use the power effectively for God's glory.

So with an authentic relationship with God as He continuously spent more time with him, Jesus said, there are some demons that will only come out through prayer and fasting. This is sacrificing for the sake of others unto God. When you build this kind of relationship with Him you have that kind of authority from Him! In the gospel of Luke it says that Jesus gave his apostles power and authority. The question is why aren't more Christians walking in this power and authority? Why are we more preoccupied with power to the absence of the need to operate according to God-given authority through our intimate relationship with him? Why do we need both?

Authority was really lost by mankind in the Garden of Eden. Jesus came to give back our lost authority. Adam and Eve were given authority by God as evidenced by his command to subdue the whole earth and make it resemble the relationship he had with them in the garden. He gave them authority over all the animal kingdom when he told Adam, whatever you name each animal that will be its name. Then Satan in the form of a serpent came along and told them that they could have power if they gained knowledge. Deceiving them into believing they could have God's kind of power and authority by just eating from the wrong tree; the tree of the knowledge of good and evil. The serpent said to Adam if you eat of this tree you will become like god. You will have power and authority.

Far too many of us seek power from knowledge taken from the tree of good and evil, while never quite committing ourselves obediently to the tree of life through an intimate and personal relationship with Christ. That allows us to enjoy the grace, extend the glory and establish the throne of God's kingdom in our lives.

Many people mistakenly think that dealing with our adversary requires some deep level of knowledge and super-spirituality. Jesus identified Satan as the 'father of lies," the master of deception. As such, it is the truth of the Word of God that dispels and expels his lies. While many of the devil's devices may appear complex, breaking them is scripturally quite simple. Faith in the supremacy and sufficiency of Jesus' name (Mark 11:22-24), confidence in the power of His atoning blood (Revelations 12:11), courage to claim and use our authority in resisting evil (Luke 10:19), and total trust in the immanent power of the Holy Spirit (Acts 10:38) will break oppression. We must focus on the truth that dealing with evil requires tools that ordinary Christians like you and I have at hand.

The Lord moves according to His purpose, if conditions for victory are met; **as we FOCUS.**

FOCUS

Stretch out

Today, we are calling each of you, Imani and our Bridge Network Partners to focus your influence on the mission or the unique purpose for your life and to commit to stretching your faith and not becoming comfortable with just "eating the popcorn" at the car dealership without "getting the keys" that open the door to what you want in life or using those keys to close and lock the door on the past that is hindering your future.

Pick an age, any age. Pick a culture, any culture. Pick a time, pick a place and then pick a person. Whoever they are, wherever they are, and whenever they are, the same questions haunt them: Who am I? Why do I exist? What will make me happy? Do I matter? The question of what should I focus on and can I commit to stretching in such a way that I fulfill the mission God created me for is a constant challenge to those called to kingdom purpose and life in Christ.

Those are the eternal questions. And their answers have eternal ramifications. They determine how we live and what we love. They shape the choices we make, the work we do and the time we spend. They give life, and they take life. They bring into focus what we are to be and do; and will cause our life to stretch in order to fulfill what we are called to do.

That is why it's imperative that we find the right answers. And there are right answers. Not just good answers, but the answers, true answers, answers that always and everywhere give peace, happiness and life. And where can we find those answers? A long time ago I noticed a note on someone's office wall saying: "It is impossible to do God's work without God's power." I believed then (and still believe now!) those words with all my heart. Yet, I often find myself becoming so busy with the things of God that I had no time left for God Himself! So weakened by a lack of focus with what power was I really attempting to so passionately focus my attention?

Too often I have become spiritually dry while doing God's work; especially when I focus on things, people and purposes that don't feed my faith but increase my doubts with their distractions and divisive comments, purposes and plans. I end up asking myself isn't my life supposed to be like a well-watered garden according to Isaiah 58:11? I know when I don't focus on what God is up to in the earth and what He has purposed for me to do as I join Him in what He is doing that I had to change. Yet, I still struggle at times to keep God Himself practically at the top of my priority list so that I won't lose focus and stop committing to stretching my faith. It is truly unfulfilling to just enjoy the temporary conveniences or thus "enjoying the popcorn at the car dealership while never receiving the keys to any of the new cars being displayed."

Can you identify with my frustration? The question for me is always do I want to grab all the opportunities to serve God that are available or do I want to focus on what God is doing around me, in me or through me? In the end you find reaching for everything available only makes you have no time to sit at the feet of Jesus focusing on Him. Are you tempted to serve God in your own power? Is it difficult for you to say "no" when a worthy project, activity or opportunity comes up - even when you know saying "yes" will be at the expense of your focus, or your opportunity to stretch your faith through a personal relationship with God? What is it that

God wants for you that causes you to stretch but not reach for everything you think you can do, while missing what is essential as you focus on God?

I believe that the only reason why Christians fail is broken focus! We as believers are on a mission for God. Together we work toward His kingdom program here on earth. We each are responsible for our part in that mission. When we discover what that personal mission is, we must give it our focus in order to maximize our influence and we must stretch out to accomplish the task.

Therefore for me, the theology of focus is the truth that I should focus my influence where God has designed and sent me. I cannot remember anyone telling me that. I probably came upon it out of burnout when I attempted to take on too many things. Or I was simply frustrated by taking on ministry and activities for which I was not designed.

Mission is God's overarching unique purpose for your life. It is the big picture of what God has called you to uniquely contribute with the life He has given you. It is a broad umbrella that covers your entire life, both career and personal. Some use the term "calling" and others use the word "vision for your life" for the same concept. So whether it is your calling or your vision our focus in life becomes the mission that we have. Therefore to fulfill the mission of your unique purpose we must stretch and adjust everything in our lives to fulfill the mission. That is the kind of mission we are talking about here. Whatever we are doing momentarily as jobs the day will come when we will no longer have the job but the mission will continue.

For example, roles such as wife or mother, father or husband, or even Christian singer or athlete even the role of preacher or teacher—when we see our missions in this light, we are in trouble because those are roles that may or may not stay with us. If we can lose the role because of death or estrangement or other loss, we lose the mission and our life-purpose. If you have seen yourself for instance not only in terms of your motherhood, or titles given to you then like so many among us you would not be lost, feeling purposeless because your children are now grown and out of the house or you no longer have the title that was giving your purpose.

Vision focuses on results while mission focuses on actions. You need vision to accomplish the mission. I am defining vision here as a picture of the future in a particular sphere of life. When I think of mission, I think of Noah who was called to be a witness of God's truth. As he was building the ark, he told them of the coming judgment; yet, there were no results. No one came to repentance before God. It can be awful frustrating when people look at their vision of what you should be accomplishing instead of appreciating that you are faithfully stretching out your faith in fulfillment of a Godly mission. Only eight were initially influenced by his mission, his sons and their wives responded and were saved from the flood. Noah became a witness to his own generation and to all of us who have followed. My question continues to be . . . "are you one of the eight?' Are you focused on the mission and stretching your faith out to fulfill it or are you just trying to catch the vision while looking at the results?

In this way we see that mission is not about results. How do you find your mission in life? One writer wrote it this way, "As the stone does not always know what ripples it has caused in the pond whose surface it impacts, so neither we nor those who watch our life will always know what we have achieved by our life and by our Mission. It may be that by the grace of God we helped bring about a profound change for the better in the lives of other souls around us, but it also may be that this takes place beyond our sight, or after we have gone on. And we may never know what we have accomplished, until we see him face-to-face after this life is past."

To me this is Imani 2.0 and the importance of focus as we bridge ourselves to the mission of Christ. We ought never to forget the stone of faith dropped into the waters of life providing for us definition and purpose thus giving vision to where we come from but ought to stretch our faith and always give praises to the bridges that by their commitment to the mission now have carried us over. We have become a part of the ripple as we now stretch our faith as a nurturing network to have an impact in our generation.

Mission as defined this way does not change. It is given by God as a life-purpose. If it were defined by roles or jobs or results, it would change. We may not understand what it is or even define it well, but it is God's purpose for your life as a believer.

Richard Nelson Bolles defines mission this way: "to exercise that Talent which you particularly came to earth to use—your greatest gift, which you most delight to use, in the place(s) or setting(s) which God has caused to appeal to you the most, and for those purposes which God most needs to have done in the world."

Jesus gave several mission-type statements throughout his life. I found several that I would call mission-type statements.

1. Mt. 9:10; Luke 5:32 "For I did not come to call the righteous, but sinners."

2. Mt. 20:28; Mark 10:45 "The Son of Man did not come to be served but to serve, and to give his life as a ransom for many."

3. Luke 19:10 "For the Son of Man came to seek and to save the lost."

4. John 9:34 "For judgment I have come into this world, so that those who do not see may gain their sight, and the ones who see may become blind."

5. John 12:47 "I have not come to judge the world, but to save the world."

6. John 18:37 "For this reason I was born, and for this reason I came into the world—to testify to the truth."

7. John 10:10 "I came that they might have life and might have it abundantly."

Although Jesus described His mission in several ways, depending upon the situation and the audience, they involve similar ideas. He came to save people and to serve them by giving His life for them and by preaching the truth to them. We see that Jesus focused His influence in the area of His mission and not the vision of results.

Luke 4:42-44 "And when day came, He departed and went to a lonely place; and the multitudes were searching for Him, and came to Him, and tried to keep Him from going away from them. But He said to them, 'I must preach the kingdom of God to the other cities also, for I was sent for this purpose.'" (NASB)

We are moving from the vision of forming a local congregation as a faithful living temple of Christ to becoming a bridge that allows us to stretch our faith to go forward and fulfill the mission of Christ in the earth connecting our faith with God's sincere purpose for our lives and the lives of others.

Luke 9:51 "Now when the days drew near for him to be taken up, Jesus set our resolutely to go to Jerusalem." At the end of Jesus' life He was able to say in John 17:4 "I glorified you on earth by completing the work you gave me to do."

Jesus on mission did not do everything that He could have done. He didn't heal all the sick; he didn't preach to everyone; He didn't bring everyone to faith. He never traveled far from home. But He did all that He was sent to do. He completed His mission. If He had failed to focus on that mission and allowed others to distract Him, He would not have been able to fulfill what He was supposed to do.

Don't lose your focus, just stretch out! Remember we are on a mission.

FOCUS

The Treasure of Incredible Worth

An index to a man's greatness is not determined by his successes but is determined rather by the vulnerability in his tribulation. If you want to understand what you can accomplish in life you must use as the basis for your dreams your ability to overcome your adversities. When you look over your life and little things messed you up and you couldn't for the life of you get through them, then suffice it to say, your dream will probably be minimal. If in your life, problems come and they mess you up: A phone call gets you disturbed. Someone rolling their eyes at you in church gets your blood boiling over. Loses or limits make you give up and quit then you will mostly be overcome by the things of this world and the people in it to the minimization of your dreams. The reality is if you can look at your life and say I lost everything but I am still here. This is what it means to have vulnerable faith.

God is saying in this season that what you declare you will have to live! Your vulnerable faith will cause you to pay a price for what it is you say you believe. God is saying in this season so very clearly, "I will not allow preachers any longer to preach about what they themselves are not participating in or leaders to lead others where they themselves have no faith in overcoming." As those who proclaim the gospel, we are accountable for the truths we declare. The question then is this: "are we willing to pay the price for what we proclaim as truth?"

What's been passing itself off as an authentic anointing has only been gifts entertaining the people. One must be careful when answering the call of the Lord. There is truly a lot of fine print in the contract of calling and the anointing given to fulfill the assignment of the bringing forth of the Kingdom that God doesn't initially tell you about even when you are gifted. God said He would bless you and you would become rich as you encounter the Kingdom life. However, he didn't tell you about the fine print, you would lose everything before first. One never knows the price that is connected to the blessing of kingdom living or the gifts God has given to be used for His good purpose.

Sometimes in the process of pursuing God you have to get away from people that make your faith vulnerable. What is so very challenging to realize is that the greatest enemy to your calling assignment, other than yourself, might very well be those closet to you and the vulnerability of their faith. They may not be your intentional enemies who wake up each day with a design and desire to be against you. But the truth of the matter is that those closest to you who think that they are helping you are the very ones who are feeding and planting the seeds of doubt and discouragement, so much so, that you, although called and on assignment, cannot fulfill the purposes of God because of those closest to you. The saddest aspect of today's church culture is watching those who cheer the gifts but even being close don't accept the responsibility of accountability and the truth that all faith is vulnerable.

Even Jesus had to continuously rebuke those disciples that were closest to Him, even rebuking His own mother. Therefore, those being the closest to you have the most influence on your destiny. So there is the need for God to take his appointed away from all the things influencing them to make sure they realize the cost that must be paid for the calling on their lives and to bring them closer to Him to become more attuned to the things of God. One of the greatest costs of a truly anointed calling is loneliness! This is what contributed to the death of Pastor Zachary Timms and the recent failings of others who seem to be falling, failing and frustrating the body of Christ as we seek to save others while being unable it seems to solve the challenge of our own vulnerable faith.

God's purpose must be priority and if God's purpose has to wrestle with our personalities to accomplish His will then the thing that is sacrificed is our personality. Jesus concerning the personality of John the Baptist asked, "What did you go out to see?" while speaking to the Pharisees as they were trying to understand John the Baptist and his ministry. He was saying to them, 'why did you go out there to the wilderness? Did you go to hear a sermon or a song sung? Did you go to be entertained by a personality? Jesus said about the Pharisees and the religious people that "you are like children in the market place." Children don't know the difference between a valuable coat from Neiman Marcus or a sweat suit on sale at Kmart. They will rub their nasty hands on them and mishandle them both just the same. Because you see they don't understand the worth and the value of where they are.

The truth of the matter is that this generation of religious people, especially it seems, its leaders, don't seem to know the value of where they are and like children in the marketplace don't understand what is valuable and what it valueless.

What we need is a 'Price Check." We have lost sight of the value of our calling and the cost associated with having an anointing. We are living a reversed kingdom life. Instead of paying the price and making the required sacrifices, we keep attempting to reverse the charges, placing the responsibility elsewhere and putting the blame on others while foolishly trading sincere faith and focus for getting by on our personalities. Jesus never said He was raising up personalities. What He said was that He was raising a body. A body is many membered. So when we see the move of God in this season, we must understand that it will not be identified, named or claimed through being associated with any personality, organization or event. When the move of God takes place and it is asked, "Who was it that initiated these things?" It will always come back not to an individual but the true source.

Elisha who is the spiritual son of Elijah received a double portion. That means he has twice as much anointing as Elijah had. He does twice the number of miracles, twice the demonstration of the power of God and becomes an even more prolific prophet because he prophesied in the king's house where as Elijah operated in the wilderness. The bible says that when the king called for Elisha he said, "go find Elisha who poured water on the hands of Elijah." (2 Kings 3:11)

Elisha was greater than Elijah; but he will always be remembered as the one who poured water on his spiritual father's hands. There is something about a generation of the church that now doesn't want the business card or the notoriety associated with the prophets of personality. But instead want only to be remembered as the one who ministered to their Father." But the hour is coming and now is when the true worshipers will worship the Father in spirit and in truth, for the Father is seeking such to worship Him. (John 4:23)

The only way you can worship in spirit and truth is when you are willing to sacrifice you! We are the temple of the Holy Spirit; the bible says in the Old Testament that in the temple there was a morning sacrifice and an evening sacrifice. If Jesus was the morning sacrifice, then as a living temple, we now are the evening sacrifice. We therefore must sacrifice as the temple in order to establish the authority of God's "cathedra," or throne. What we sacrifice is who we are as we obediently commit ourselves as servants to the purpose of the fulfillment of God's calling on our lives and ministry. This takes Vulnerable Faith and Sacrifice to become who He is **as a Treasure of Incredible Worth.**

The Apostle Paul says, "It is no longer I who lives but Christ lives in me." (Galatians 2:20). As his living temple we are united by faith to Christ in His death, and we have died to the old life and have risen to a new life, a life blessed to be fully expressed in kingdom living. When we come to this place even when there is a semblance of success it will not feed our ego because we have become selfless.

So with our elevation, God has us on the path of apostles in this season. Our calling is to covenant not to build our self up. The new buzz word is who is your covering or who are you associated with? As we come together as a Bridge Network Covenant Fellowship we believe absolutely in being connected. But it is NOT the popular approach of fellowships in this season where writing of checks, receiving someone's tape series and coming to pastors conferences once a year. We pass this off as being connected, but the truth is it still doesn't mean that there is a connection at all.

There has to be something more; when I connect to something there is a source of supply that transcends what is seen as this prevailing approach of the day. It is like when trying to hook up your laptop while in a church but you can't because you don't have the password or key into the local network. Though there is information available and you are in the proximity of the information, the truth is just because you are around someone doesn't mean that you are connected to them.

Therefore the effort of expectation focuses more on the effort from us to believe and walk out God's promise more than the expectation that the promise would manifest. Our case study of the life of Abraham shows that God's promises are packed with His word to carry out what is promised. God appears, he commands, he promises this former idol worshipper a life blessed beyond comprehension. God doesn't show up with a "bag of blessings" or give him tricks to perform just His word.

I am humbled by the revelation that my expectation of God is commensurate with my vulnerable faith in Him. It is never an issue about what I expect from God; what is always at issue is my effort toward that expectation. The Apostle Paul says in Romans 4 that "Abraham stumbled not at the promise of God because he was fully persuaded that what God promised He was able to perform". His confidence in God was assured by his effort to trust God for his promise which is "The Treasure of Incredible Worth." Our expectation is linked to God's promise! If Abraham failed in his effort to trust God with his vulnerable faith (offering up Isaac, interceding for Lot, believing he could produce the promise through a barren wife etc) then his expectation of God would equally be diminished. Abraham put forth 25yrs of effort to get one promise manifested. He never stopped believing even though he at times through his vulnerable faith faltered. Still he is the Father of Faith. He never diminished his effort to trust, obey, believe and walk out what God had commanded even though his expectation had no manifestation.

Other biblical characters like Noah, Hannah and Moses portray similar focus of effort proving that they had great expectation of the Lord. Even with vulnerable faith they chose to make the sacrifice. Build an ark in expectation of a flood; put forth an effort in prayer for a son when you are barren. Effort is the evidence of faith. We will always do what we believe no matter if it's the right or wrong thing...we believe it. Moses leads millions of Jews into a desert in expectation of finding a promise land but their vulnerable faith causes most to miss the promise. Does your effort tell the story of your faith or lack thereof? What are you willing in expectation to sacrifice?

The effort of expectation requires diligent movement towards the expectation of the promise even when there maybe no evidence of it being fulfilled.

Great Expectation

    Little Effort = DISAPPOINTMENT!

Vulnerable faith

    Great sacrifice = Connection to a Treasure of Incredible Worth

It's perfectly alright to have great expectation from the Lord. It's not alright to have little effort, no accountability or lack of sacrifice. You can have anything you want for yourself and your life if you CHOOSE to participate in it and are willing to be held accountable.

It has been said many times by many great thinkers and proclaimers of truth that great achievement is usually born of great sacrifice, and is never the result of selfishness, it claims or focus. We must learn to focus more faithfully on our purpose and learn to trust in the Lord and cherish our visions and our dreams more faithfully, as they are the promises of our soul, the blueprints of our ultimate achievements.

John in Revelation 1:9 said he was a partner in suffering, and it is through physical or mental pain, disappointments, frustrations, and sorrows, loneliness and the struggle of striving that the means by which we either become great and grow in grace and in knowledge or go down in the flames of permanent failure is realized. The determining factor as to which of these two circumstances one embraces depends entirely upon their focus and mental attitude toward them. Can we pay the price and make the sacrifice in order to receive the treasure of incredible worth?

To one person they may become stumbling blocks. However, for yet another person...they become stepping-stones to a higher dimension of life, from which one may become the recipients of God's blessing or favor. The greatest obstacles we face in reaching personal goals: fear, procrastination, anger, and jealousy, are tools of the Devil. These hidden methods of control can lead us to ruin.

What are the tools of the devil? "Lest Satan should get an advantage of us: for we are not ignorant of his devices." (2 Corinthians 2:11) Are you ignorant of the devil's devices? Don't be, learn them, know them, be on guard for them, resist them, and defeat the devil. God promises that if we submit ourselves to God and if we resist the devil, that the devil will flee from us (James 4:7). As believers, we must know the devil's devices; the tools the devil uses, so that he cannot take advantage of us.

Always remember that Satan, the devil, is always seeking, searching out those who he can deceive, trick, destroy and kill (1 Peter 5:8). The main goal of Satan, with all his tricks and devices, is to separate us from God for all eternity. Satan is the enemy of God. Satan, the devil, is the adversary, the enemy of all believers of Christ Jesus. Being our enemy we must arm ourselves every day, we must know the devil's tricks and tools, the devices Satan uses to trip us up and uses to deceive us and uses to try and destroy our relationship with God.

Some of the tools of the devil are: hate, selfishness, pride, unforgiveness, ungodly thoughts, lying, uncaring, tempting God, blaspheming God, false doctrines, fear, defeat, false guilt, idolatry, worry, false love, covetousness, shame, false glory, material possessions, fame, and sin. All of this makes our faith vulnerable by their constant attacks on our very best efforts and expectation of receiving God's promise. That's why people close to you make you so vulnerable. In their access to you their faith is vulnerable to the purposes of Satan and not God.

We all must be introduced to a power that is greater than poverty, lack of education a power greater than our superstitions and fears; a power that overcomes barren situations and the accusations of the enemy. We have the power to take possession of our own minds and direct it to whatever ends we may desire. This profound power is a gift of God and is one of the greatest gifts given to us by God. The truth is that it is the only thing that we have complete and unchallengeable control and direction of. As a people when we focus our mind on our minimums and limitations, on things that hinder and create unknown realistic poverty, and unproductive processing of information, the result is we have directed our own minds to the attraction of products of undesirable consequences of our own thoughts and circumstances or those closest to you. Because it really is true that whatever your mind feeds upon your mind attracts to you.

Therefore, all success begins with Focus. A definite purpose that has a clear vision of what you truly desire out of life. We all begin life able to direct our minds to whatever ends we may choose. All life consists of choices and chances, possibilities and penalties. When we focus on desiring God's blessings what do we mean? "The blessings of the Lord maketh one rich and adds no sorry to it." What does it mean to have God's blessing on your life? God truly is able to make all things work together for our good (Romans 8:28). Our attitude is so important. A positive and faith-filled attitude will help keep us in the flow of God's "in-house" blessing, even when outward circumstances seem barren or unpromising.

Rather than allowing outward prosperity or wealth to determine our attitudes, we must realize that the inner blessing of the fruit of the Spirit is a **treasure of incredible worth.**

FOCUS

Giving Your Heart A Home!

Here is a truth that may help some of you to more effectively focus. Always be careful of what you say because people may not always hear when you say what you said. They may not always hear what you say you thought you said. There are some technicalities that count.

For instance *Consecration and Dedication* are two different things. So what we must work hard at as leaders, especially ministry leaders, is to:

1. Work hard at sending the right signals.
2. Remember you are always sending a signal,
3. Hard as you try to send a clear signal, don't forget that somebody will always misunderstand the signal you send.

Likewise, seeing and focusing are two different things. As is living a life and living a focused life are not the same either. There is an element of our vision that we affirm, we believe in, we are trusting God to do, it is important to us but still may not have happened yet for many of you. Though the signal has been sent, though we see the glory of God appearing in our worship services each week, we all have not always heard the signal, seen the significance of the concepts, or received the blessings that have been offered. Thus the vision is unclear and the effectiveness of the focus is questionable.

It maybe very clear to you but not observable to others! So we must focus and focus others to hear what we say with clarity and see the vision effectively in order to live it out and enjoy, extend and establish it in the lives we share as a family of faith and body of Christ. As a "Family of Faith" there are some things we want to articulate as vision and focus on appropriately as a ministry. The ladder of success begins with focusing in several ways:

> First on those who can be seen as first comers who begin a new community.
>
> Then the enjoyment which is developed by an affinity group whose faith over time comes into focus as they share life together.
>
> Then as they focus – they fellowship and faithfully begin to share life together as they become moved by purpose as a caring community.
>
> An intimate climate of shared synergy is created.
>
> The life development process becomes a point of focus as we become open to being equipped to take our place in the equipping community.
>
> Becoming as yielded leadership a leadership community with tiers of leadership and a commitment and dedication to nurturing and extending the grace of God to all we come in contact with.

All this takes Focus:

- FAITH
- OBEDIENCE
- COMMITMENT
- UNITY
- SERVANTHOOD

Thus we begin living the Focused Life. As we step into a life of Focus, we must never forget where we are and don't stay where you are. If you can see no further than where you are you cannot see far enough. On the other hand no matter how far you get from where you are never forget where you are now. Whether you are the new community, the faith community, becoming a part of the caring community, beginning to experience and express the intimate climate of shared synergy, or developing into an equipped and equipping part of the equipped community, or have yielded enough to take your place in the tiers of leadership. There must be clarity in the vision. There must be a focus in order to live the Focused Life as a servant of Christ.

God may take you light years from where you've been or even where you are, but never forget you've been there. **An important question becomes: HOW FAR CAN I SEE FROM WHERE I AM?**

Sometimes, the question is not so much 'how far can I see?" But the better question is "what direction am I looking in?" All of this is related to VISION.

The prophet Habakkuk raises the question of vision in his short prophetic book. The question is not so much – "how our churches are doing?" but HOW CAN WE SEE OUR CHURCHES DOING? – WHAT DO I SEE THE CHURCH BECOMING?

MOVING FROM A TEMPLE TO A CATHEDRAL! WHERE THE THRONE OF GOD IS ESTABLISHED, THE GRACE OF GOD IS ENJOYED, AND THE GLORY OF GOD IS EXTENDED . . . calls for each of us to receive and experience this vision as we focus our lives to be used as vessels for the Lord's good purpose.

Habakkuk 2:2: "Then the Lord answered me and said "Write the Vision and make it plain on tablets that he may run who reads it." Write the Vision: Chapter 2 verse 2 does not begin in chapter 2 verse 2, it begins in chapter 1 verse 1. Chapter 2 verse 2 talks about "Vision." Chapter 1 verse 1 talks about "Burden."

Before you see a vision "YOU WILL HAVE A BURDEN." The clarity of a vision, <u>AND THE VALIDITY OF A VISION</u> – *relates to the clarity and validity of a burden.* **The Focused Life is life lived with a burden.**

Burden has to do with 'Motive."

Vision has to do with

- Method – (what I do)
- Means –(how I do it)
- Manner – (the way I do it)

At any given point of the revelation and the manifestation of vision there will be a revelation and manifestation of a burden. In other words, no matter what you see or what you are trying to do at some **point your real motive is going to come out!**

Burden can often be highly disguised and camouflaged. Motive can be covered up a lot and one can fake it. You just can't fake it all the time. So therefore the question that arises out of vision is: WHY AM I DOING THIS? WHY DO I PUT UP WITH THIS? WHAT IS THE VALIDATION? WHAT LEGITIMIZES ME GOING THROUGH THIS?

Until you have asked and answered these questions you have not gone through enough to live the focused life of serving the Lord and enjoying His grace, extending His glory and establishing His throne.

Why am I putting up with this?

Why am I in this routine?

Why am I trying to do this at all?

This will always lead us back to burden.

Habakkuk 2:2 will always take me back to Habakkuk 1:1! So vision demands that if you are "Preparing to sit at the table of God's favor (captured, consecrated, and dedicated for the Master's use", or understanding the relevance of having a perspective of living life beyond your comma and into the conjunction of "But God" as you pursue the mysteries of godly perfection (which is God active in our lives); then you are in a position to FOCUS (faith, obedience, commitment, unity, and servant-hood) and available to move, along with others committed to enjoying his grace, extending His glory and establishing the throne of God's authority in the earth.

But, if you are doing this for any burden that is not of God the vision will not be of God. A focused life is a life of Servant-hood! Focused life as a concept means restoring intimacy with God, nurturing and developing sensitivity as participants in the shared story of our worship and work as servant leaders, and sharing responsibility for the created communities of grace called churches as we walk out and work through our faith synergistically or interdependently as sincere servants or Disciples of Christ.

To step into the benefits and the ability to enjoy this life you must focus your untamed life. That's what Jesus came to give us. In John 10:10 he said, *"I have come that you may LIFE, and have it to the full.* The church very seldom talks about this life and we want to talk about the Focused Life in this way. In other words LIFE according to Jesus, the Focused Life! Or Life focused on fulfilling our Godly purpose.

In John 14:6 Jesus says, *I am the way and the truth and the LIFE. No one comes to the Father except through me.* Jesus is into life. Jesus did not come to this earth to start a new religion or a thing called Christianity. Jesus is much bigger than that. His goal was not to fill up our time with meetings and religious activity to keep us all out of trouble. Jesus' focus is much larger than that.

Jesus came to this earth to renew and redeem all things. He's out to reverse the curse and put an end to death and destruction and all the pain that sin brings. He's out to establish his kingdom in this world and finally see God's will done on earth as it is in heaven. His mission is universal and his focus cosmic in scope. He wants to make all things new and that includes you and that includes me. And he's not going to stop until he gets it done. And he will get it done. You can count on that.

In Matthew 19:28-30 Jesus said to his disciples, "*Truly I tell you, at the renewal of all things, when the Son of Man sits on his glorious throne, you who have followed me will also sit on twelve thrones judging the twelve tribes of Israel.* [29]*And everyone who has left houses or brothers or sisters or father or mother or wife or children or fields for my sake will receive a hundred times as much and will inherit eternal life.* [30]*But many who are first will be last and many who are last will be first.*"

Following Jesus is not about religion. It's about reality. It's about FOCUS (faith, obedience, commitment, unity and servant-hood). It's about lining ourselves up with the way things really are. Following Jesus is the best possible way to live. It's the greatest return on investment we can ever make with our lives. It's worth every minute of it and every sacrifice it demands.

Our focus as a church exists to be a biblical community helping people become fully devoted followers of Jesus Christ, who make a difference in this world.

Jesus calls us to _be_ disciples and to _make_ disciples; to enjoy the grace and then extend the Glory by establishing Jesus' authority on earth. The Greek word for disciple is mathetes. It's a rich word that comes from the Greek verb manthano which means "to learn." So mathetes literally means "learner, student, apprentice, one who follows and imitates a teacher."

Jesus invites us to be his apprentices, his followers, his imitators. He's the teacher. We're the students. He's the rabbi or teacher. We're the learners, and a real life of focus comes when we imitate and follow him because he is the way, the truth, and the LIFE. Being a disciple of Jesus doesn't start with joining the church as a member or going out and saving the world, being a disciple of Jesus starts with coming to Jesus and listening to Him. He extends the invitation to come to him every single day.

So we start the Focused Life with Jesus' words in Matthew 11:28, *Come to me, all you who are weary and burdened, and I will give you rest.* Does anyone here feel weary and burdened? Does anyone here need rest? Not more responsibility. Not more rules to follow. Not more rituals to keep. Not more reasons to feel guilty and bad and stressed out and like we can't measure up. *COME TO ME, all you who are weary and burdened and I will give you rest.*

Jesus is always asking us to come to him. Even if we've responded before, we're invited to come again. Even if we're too tired to walk, we can crawl to Jesus on our hands and knees, exhausted and wounded and defeated and beaten down by the stress and the demands of life. He still invites us to sit at the table of His favor to enjoy the grace, extend the glory and establish the throne. It doesn't matter how long you've been away. He says, "Come to me." It doesn't matter if you've never come before. He says, "Come to me." It's an open invitation to be understood and embraced by Jesus. *Come to me, ALL you who are weary and burdened, and I will give you rest.* It doesn't matter who you are...your age, your gender, your race, your past, your income or experience. It doesn't matter if you're Baptist or Church of God in Christ. The invitation is open to all who are humble enough to admit they need Jesus.

But Jesus says more than just "come to me," as wonderful as that is. He says something else, something so comforting, so compelling that we just want to collapse in his strong arms. *Come to me, all you who are weary and burdened, and I WILL GIVE YOU REST.* The Greek word for rest literally means "rest, refreshment." *Come to me, all you who are weary and burdened, and I WILL GIVE YOU REST. Take my yoke upon you and learn from me, for I am gentle and humble in heart, and you will find REST FOR YOUR SOULS.*

It's one thing to find rest for our bodies. That's important. It's great when we can take a midday nap or sit in a Jacuzzi or get a solid night's sleep. But even more important than to have rest for our bodies is to have rest for our souls because it's the inner struggle, the inner turmoil, the fear and the anxiety that life creates that can wear our souls and intimidate us so much more quickly than the fatigue in our bodies.

Rest for our souls, rest from the pressures of our jobs, our families, our finances, our relationships, our commitments, and our responsibilities. Rest ... like no other rest we've ever experienced. That's what Jesus offers us. Sounds great doesn't it? Who wouldn't want that rest? But here's the twist. With Jesus there's always a twist. He says, *Come to me, all you who are weary and burdened, and I will give you rest. ²⁹TAKE MY YOKE upon you and learn from me, for I am gentle and humble in heart, and you will find rest for your souls. ³⁰FOR MY YOKE is easy and my burden is light.*

We find rest for our souls when we yoke up with Jesus. What's a yoke? Well, when we think of a yoke we probably think of an egg yolk, the yellow part of an egg that feeds the embryo and is surrounded by the egg white. That is spelled yolk. That's not the yoke Jesus is talking about here. The yoke Jesus is talking about is a wooden beam that connects two oxen together and it helps them focus. In Jesus' day, in the land of Israel at least, that's how farming was done. Two oxen were paired together for maximum effectiveness.

A young, wild, inexperienced ox was linked to an older more seasoned, mature ox to be trained how to pull a plough or how to tread out the grain. The experienced ox would know where to walk and how fast to go and how to relate to the farmer and how to get the job done. Kind of like a personal trainer. But the younger, wilder ox didn't know how to do those things. And so at first it would strain at the yoke and try to go its own way. Or it might try to rush ahead or lag behind the lead ox, but before long it would be exhausted and have a very sore neck!

But eventually the younger ox would learn the ways of the leader and be much more productive and have much less pain. In other words he would develop focus. *Take my yoke upon you, Jesus says, and LEARN FROM ME.* That word for "learn" is the Greek word mathete. It's the word for disciple as we have previously stated. Jesus is saying, *Take my yoke upon you and be discipled by me and you will find rest for your souls.*

We can't go out and make disciples of others if we're not allowing Jesus to make disciples of us. And that starts when we yoke ourselves to Jesus and focus on his teaching. When we focus: with faith, obedience, commitment, unity and servant-hood we begin to live the Focused Life of a disciple of Christ.

In fact, in Jesus' day a rabbi's teaching was called his yoke. Different rabbis had different ways of interpreting the Jewish law. And when you followed a certain rabbi that you believed was interpreting the Scriptures correctly you were taking up that rabbi's yoke. You were linking yourself to him and his teaching. As we take our place in the life of faith we are yoked to Christ and the vision He has given me to give to you so we live a focused life of Godly purpose and promise. Life according to Jesus is a yoke! Not a joke. A yoke! And the truth is we are all yoked to somebody or something. And that yoke will either bring us rest or get us stressed. That yoke will either bring us life or bring us death. Life is going to be hard whether we're yoked to Jesus or not because we live in a broken world. Life was hard for Jesus, but in the midst of it all we can find rest for our souls as he did.

The choice is ours. Jesus is asking us to come to him, to link up with him, to learn from him, and to be discipled by him. The creator of the universe, the King of Kings and the Lord of Lords, the all knowing, all powerful, almighty, all loving God who describes himself as gentle and humble in heart. And that's what he wants to teach us to be as well. Gentle and humble in heart. Are you ready to discover that life?

An author composed a song from Matthew 11:28-30 called "Give Your Heart a Home." He wrote it as if it were being sung by Jesus to people who are burned out and weighed down by life...maybe the way you're feeling right now. The lyrics go like this... "I hear your hollow laughter, your sighs of secret pain. Pretending and inventing, just to hide your shame. Plastic smiles and faces, blinking back the tears, Empty friends and places, all magnify the fears. If you're tired and weary, weak and heavy-laden, I can understand how, it feels to be alone. I will take your burden, if you'll let me love you. I'll wrap my arms around you and give your heart a home. It hurts to watch you struggle, and try so hard to win; you trade your precious birthright, for candy-coated sin. Wasting precious moments, restless and confused, building up defenses, for fear that you'll be used. Take my yoke upon you, walk here by my side. Let me heal your heartaches, dry the tears you've cried. Never will I leave you, never turn away. I'll keep you through the darkness, lead you through the day. If you're tired and weary, weak and heavy-laden, I can understand how, it feels to be alone. I will take your burden, if you'll let me love you. I'll wrap my arms around you and give your heart a home."

With your Focused Life, begin to "Enjoy the grace, extend the glory and establish the throne! Giving your heart a home!

FOCUS

Till Death Do Us Part
Or Until I'm Tired of Trying

Many of you have begun to come to me regarding your relationships, preparation for marriage and desire for better information; which will allow for taking a more biblical approach for your happiness in marriage. One of the most damaging insights people have is that there is no need to understand what marriage and relationships are truly all about. "Why do you have to work on a marriage some have asked? If you love each other, isn't that all that matters?"

Well, the truth of the matter is as we look at 50% and higher divorce rates, even Christian marriages with the second and even the third marriage having a higher rate of divorce than the previous one. It is clear that the role of marriage in this society is coming under a tremendous attack and now even more so in the church.

The department of motor vehicles in our state will not issue you a driver's license until you can prove to them (on a test, administered in a crowded building by less-than-happy DMV employees, usually) that you not only know how to read all road signs, but that you can also interpret what they mean. The DMV wants to know that you are competent enough to obey posted signs—signs that indicate laws that were established for our protection. But we offer a license to many unfocused people who then proceed to drive the institution of marriage off a cliff.

Likewise, God has established laws in the universe He created. His laws are for our benefit and blessing, to protect us and keep us from harming others and ourselves. He has given us signs that He cares for us by establishing laws governing our behavior. He's given us the Bible, the church, pastors and teachers and leaders, our parents, coaches, and the experience of mature people to warn us.

If we ignore the signs, we pay the price; just as ignoring road signs could cost us a speeding ticket or a head-on collision. It could cost us a fine, our privilege of driving, or even our life. So it's much better to read the signs and obey them. Or as it has been so pointedly said many times by those of us who've experienced not obeying the signs; "You better check yourself before you wreck yourself and hurt someone else." His law says, if you enter into the covenant of marriage it is till death do you part and not until you're tired of trying! Or have suffered an accident because of poor marriage conditions, negligence or faulty marriage maintenance, preparation or unfaithful focus.

There is so much unhappiness in the home! Homes that should be a bit of heaven on earth have become, in a large sense, a bit of pure misery. The divorce courts are filled to capacity with people mumbling about their inability to obtain happiness. Little children are left stunned and defeated by another broken home. What has happened to the couple that just a short time ago pledged, "Till death do us part?"

Now . . .

- The planned happiness is gone.

- The home is broken.

- The children are left without a mother or a daddy.

- The truth is that God has not intended for this to happen.

Why do so many homes and marriages break up today? Many reasons could be listed, but I believe the primary reason homes and marriages break up, is because of a lack of serious PREPARATION, FOUNDATION and FOCUS! Like everything else of importance, marriage must be prepared for, must be entered into on a firm and carefully constructed foundation and must endure with a healthy and Covenantal FOCUS (Faith, obedience, commitment, unity and servant-hood).

We sometimes forget in the "everydayness" of life that God cares more about our character than He does about our comfort. And as we marry, we continually find areas of our lives together that God wants to teach us about what it means to love someone sacrificially. Our marriages are to be visible pictures of Christ's sacrificial love for His church. And in order to do that, we must "die to self" every day of our lives so Christ may live in and through us.

God chose the Garden of Eden to institute marriage, and His Word abounds with both promises and warnings to safeguard the family. A marriage established and guided by Biblical standards has the potential of such blessedness that it can be compared to Christ's relationship with His beloved church (Ephesians 5:22-23). At the same time, violation of Scriptural standards brings pain and guilt producing consequences.

Yet, marriage as an institution is currently receiving numerous attacks and far too many are now suffering and on life-support from mismanagement and an unfocused lack of commitment. Think back for a moment and consider the training and teaching you received in preparation for marriage. If you were like most, you will agree that there was no formal training. That is, you didn't go to college or a technical school to be trained and certified as a husband or wife. There is no diploma or certification that qualified us to be married. Most didn't submit to marriage counseling and the marriage counseling you received was inadequate for the divine purpose for which marriage was instituted in the first place.

Far too many of us participated in a wedding only to find ourselves in a marriage we were never prepared for. We ate the cake but cursed the marriage with a lack of focus. We never checked what we individually were bringing to the altar and when we got home we dumped our trash out on one another and our marriage suffered as a result of our lack of care, commitment and consideration.

We all bring emotional baggage; garbage from our past, deficits with limited assets into the marriage relationship. These deficits, and don't just look at your mate here but turn the mirror on yourself, are emotional deficits (lack of emotional stability in a certain area caused by some past negative experience or some past negative event) that if not addressed and properly handled hinder your ability to love and have a good relationship.

However, of all the choices we make in our lifetime, the selection of our spouse and decisions we make on how to be a husband or wife, are the most profound and have the most far-reaching implications. Churches themselves are made up of families; some from broken and mismanaged marriages, blended families, single parents, mostly female headed, absentee father families. Children (other people) will come from those decisions and the process continues from generation to generation. In fact, we exist today because of decisions made by our parents, people who entered into marriage with a vow of faith, obedience, commitment, unity, and servant-hood with or without a vow of fidelity toward one another "till death do us part".

This brings me to my initial point about the subject of marriage. Our parents have had a profound impact on us with regard to marriage. It was our parents that served as our primary teachers in preparing us for marriage and even the nature of relationships. If our parent's marriage was insufficient for them, then for the most part, it provided a faulty foundation for a healthy approach to marriage for us. Just like any training course, the quality of that training has a direct impact on the success or failure of our encounters in the land of promise with regard to healthy and fulfilling relationships. If you have had no parental guidance, marriage preparation or a healthy model is it any wonder the quality of our relationships become far to challenging for us to accomplish the desired results in them?

But our parents are not the only resource to prepare us for marriage. The Bible has a lot to say about marriage. In fact, the very institution of marriage originates from the Bible. Marriage is a great mystery the bible says in Ephesians 5:32. There has been a world full of poets, philosophers and songwriters attempting to explain love and marriage to us. But this mystery described in the bible far surpasses them all. If you were to ask any married person why they put up with their spouses' mistakes and shortcomings, they would give the same answer regardless of gender; "Because, I love them." But the mystery of marriage is that it is not based on love but commitment. Love will go up and down, be hot and cold, come and go! But marriage is about a commitment till death do us part.

Now don't get it wrong, because love covers a multitude of sins. This is the same simple answer God continues to deal with us. He loves us, and His love covers the multitude of our sins. True marriage is first and foremost a spiritual union between an imperfect man and an imperfect woman established by a covenant or promise of commitment between the two. The commitment to this covenant between the married couple causes a spiritual change to take place where the two become one flesh. *"But at the beginning of creation God made them male and female. For this reason a man will leave his father and mother and be united to his wife, and the two will become one flesh. So they are no longer two, but one flesh. Therefore what God has joined together, let no one separate."* (Mark 10:6-9 NIV).

This is why one must be careful about attempting to fulfill just the legal aspects and requirements of marriage by going to the Elvis Presley Chapel of Love to get married. You see, complying with the laws of the state doesn't affect the spiritual change necessary for the foundation of marriage to accomplish its divine purpose. The law does not care if you have really committed to the man or woman you wish to marry. It now doesn't care if you are married to the same gender. The law is only concerned with you completing the legal procedure to be married in that particular state. Fulfill the states requirements and legally anyone qualified or not can be married under the law. It foundationally does not require spiritual union, which as Christians we believe is the problem with many marriages today.

It is truly amazing how many people try to justify a sinful relationship in order to avoid spiritual responsibilities. Even spiritual unions are insufficient if we do not follow the laws regarding marriage where we live. So a couple can be bound spiritually, but not completely married. If the two commit to each other and are joined spiritually as if there were no government, but do not satisfy the local legal requirements for marriage then they are driving illegally . . . and are not married. A Christian marriage is established by the spiritual and legal union. A man and woman cannot live together and claim to be married. The fact that they do so without going through the legal process demonstrates that they are not committed to each other.

Likewise, our parents and basic biblical instruction about marriage are our primary sources of reference for marriage. Without either why would you believe that you could drive the marriage safely without crashing it with the faulty foundation and focus you entered into it with?

But also, have you ever even considered the teaching we have concerning marriage given in the Bible? Let me explain a bit more. Since our parents are our primary examples, have you considered what our parents in the Bible teach us about marriage? Which parents am I referring to? Adam and Eve, Abraham and Sarah, Isaac and Rebekah, and Jacob and his wives Leah and Rachel, have a lot to teach us about marriage!

Numerous reasons are advanced for abandoning marriage, and all find root in a desire to be free from any external standards or restraints (i.e., God's revelation). The family (parents and children) is viewed as artificial by some who say that man's more natural living arrangement is in groups—tribes or communes. The enemies intent on reshaping society attack the family, for he recognizes it as the basic unity of a civilized culture.

To be sure, the institution of marriage is old, but that does not mean it is obsolete. Marriage was thousands of years old at Christ's first coming, but He still taught its appropriateness. "But from the beginning of creation, God made them male and female. For this cause a man shall leave his father and mother, and the two shall become one flesh ... What therefore God has joined together, let no man separate" (Mark 10:6-9). The Christian realizes he is not at liberty to tamper with God's Word to conform it to passing fads in social theories. Cultural norms must be judged by Scripture; the Scripture is not judged by our changing cultural practices or worldly ideas of cohabitation or socially engineered concepts of marriage arrangements outside of a man and a woman in covenant till death do us part.

God never intended marriage to be a test-drive relationship, but a binding pledge of permanence, patience and prayerful partnership. When the Creator established the blueprints for marriage He stated, "For this reason a man will leave his father and mother and be united to his wife, and they will become one flesh (Genesis 2:24).

God knew from the very beginning that marriage, the first institution of life, would not be about convenience, but commitment. Commitments of life changing proportions are never struggle free. They take Focus: *faith, obedience, commitment, unity and servant-hood.*

Love is an unconditional commitment to an imperfect person. Who you love determines how you have to love them! No matter the marriage or relationship problem, the foundation that sustains it is focus. Every marriage maintains its balance as the two people invested in it and focused on it shift their positions, their attitudes, and their behaviors to balance and counter one another.

So my advice today is this, if you want to know the end of anything first take a look at its beginning. A solid foundation sustains a healthy and stable structure. A weak or weakened or neglected foundation over time will bring down the best structure built on it. The single best day in every marriage is when the two people in it take responsibility for their part in making it healthy, happy and whole.

Look in the mirror and ask God today how He can use you to transform the person looking back at you. If you have let a spirit of bitterness, terrorized by the giant of intimating thoughts, manipulations, fears and frustrations into the marriage, stop asking God to change your partner and ask God to change you. Most marriages are lost because the people in them lose themselves and lost people take detours, make dangerous decisions, and have devastating consequences to their attempts to participate in God's divinely designed purpose for marriage.

The bible says, "My people are destroyed for a lack of knowledge." And so is marriage. Something happened after people walked down the aisle, thinking everything was going to be alright after that? Part of what happened was they didn't have the knowledge or focus to maintain a good relationship.

My commitment to God defines my commitment to my wife Kathy. My commitment to her then defines my commitment to everybody else outside of our relationship. So my in-laws, children, friends or church members do not come before her. The strongest natural relationship I have is with my wife and not with my homies, other preachers, you as members or my love or commitment to work; not my parents or my children. It is commitment to God first that defines my commitment to Kathy and that defines all other relationships in my life.

"For this reason a man will leave his father and mother and be united to his wife, and they will become one flesh (Genesis 2:24).

Stay Focused! It's till death do us part!

FOCUS

"Excuse Me, But Your Integrity is Showing!"

Quoting A. W. Tozer, *"God will crucify without pity those whom He desires to raise without measure!* Therefore we must FOCUS: (faith, obedience, commitment, unity and servant-hood) as we move into a "Season of Consecration" and a year of fulfilled promises as a fellowship of committed believers. The bible says, "Consecrate yourselves and be holy, because I am the LORD your God." Leviticus 20:7

George Barna predicts that 70% of the church will be worshiping in non-traditional settings within the next 20yrs. This means that churches like ours, as we move into our 14th year of ministry and our inaugural year of Episcopal covering, will become more influential than traditional churches in the future. The post-modern world and its core values have led to a distrust of authority; suspicion of structure, and an unabashed pursuit of authenticity. This has led to a distrust of the church leadership and a distancing from the religious traditions of the church. Unusual is not necessarily holy and convenient is not always consecrated.

With these things in mind, we focus on the D.N.A. of the covenant promises of this new move and covenant journey to go from a temple to a cathedral, and extending our focus as the house of God to a covenant commitment to corporately pursuing the kingdom promises through Divine Truth, Nurturing Relationships, and Apostolic Mission (D.N.A.). The core ingredients of our new church movement make us healthier and more participatory as we build a bridge of nurturing covenant that is relational, authentic and experiential, and with leadership integrity focus on fulfilling our God-given promises.

The rewards of godly leadership are so great and the responsibilities of the leader so heavy that no one can afford to take the matter lightly. A leader leads by example, whether he intends to or not. If you as a leader are not careful, your integrity will expose you for who you truly are. Sometimes standing for principles is going to cost you something. But not near as much as it will eventually cost you if you do not stand for them. A leader who stands for nothing will eventually fall for everything his integrity cannot withstand.

It is the quality of a leader's integrity that can bear to be sat on, absorb shocks, and act as a buffer, being much plagued. The wear and tear of the continual friction and trials which come to the servants of God are the greatest test of character. The character of a person is revealed in how he or she responds in moments of impossibility; when it is impossible to do in and of ones self what one is confronted with. Ultimately, it is much easier to keep your character than it is to recover it. I believe the biggest challenge in the church of today is character and the most needed aspect of that character needed is integrity.

Amid the latest ministry scandals, covenantal leaders have begun to charge pastors and church leaders with specific demands to not only avoid moral failure, but also to consecrate themselves to the commitment to leave a legacy of integrity for fulfilled promises rather than the faulty presentation of fake and failed personalities. We're now seeing many of the largest churches in America pastored by people who are living a double lifestyle, and are in need of consecration. This is a crisis. This isn't something we're dreaming up—this is the reality of where pastors and leaders are right now when it comes to the integrity of leadership in our churches.

With ministry scandals reported almost weekly and studies indicating that up to 40 percent of American pastors view pornography every day, the need for integrity among church leaders is obvious. But we must understand that leadership integrity isn't simply staying away from sexually explicit websites, but includes everything from keeping a commitment to managing church budgets to honoring a spouse. Prosperity preaching, mega church visions, and personality driven ministries are like wells drying up; and no one is looking to draw from them. Who is looking for integrity?

We are most assuredly going to lose our nation and our churches if we don't turn our pastors around, but how can we change our nation if we can't keep our word church leaders? The Apostle Paul's warning ought to be the clarion call of our day for us as church leaders; "abstain from all appearance of evil" (1 Thess. 5:22, KJV).

A lapse in watchfulness or vigilance can easily steal your integrity. When it comes to integrity, you can't watch too much. You can't be too careful when it comes to your integrity. Excuse me, but your integrity may or may not be showing. As long as more leaders fail to stay vigilant, we can expect more cultural degradation—with the outward signs of a nation and its churches no longer being blessed by God is on display all around us. "The American church is at a place where the nation has been under a judgment of God," one leading church leader said, citing the cost of leader's "hidden" sins found Ezekiel 14:8-12. Our economic and moral woes have to do with God saying, 'I cannot bless you as I have blessed you in times past unless you turn to Me.' The church cannot return to her covenantal God until the prophetic voices mount pulpits and declare a consecrated Focus on the fulfillment of Godly purpose instead of fleshly and immoral desires.

Likewise, as we contemplate the daily revelations coming from the world of professional sports regarding the use of performance enhancing drugs, it reminds us that any short-cut one takes to attain growth may compromise integrity. The local church faces a similar dilemma. A local church can grow by using any number of enhancements: for instance, by appealing to consumerism of this age, creating a "trendy" atmosphere instead of a sincere picture of worship, posturing instead of reaching out to felt needs, trying not to offend members, or by attempting to please all those people who enter the door. These "short-cut" methods to achieve church health, growth and relevance can do harm to the corporate body just like drugs can harm the individual's body.

A church that wants to obey Christ must ask some tough questions: Does our mentality or attitude compromise the integrity of the church as established by Christ? Are numbers at any cost the most important thing? Does the church want to be "bigger and better" by any means or should it be satisfied to maintain its integrity even if that means growing at a slower rate at first?

Leadership is a special call of God. Being in a leadership position in ministry is a wonderful role to have, but there are always temptations that challenge your integrity as a leader. Many have fallen into areas of sin that have destroyed their integrity and ministries. Although they are human like the rest of us, their sin causes pain not only to themselves, but also too many others. When will the church acknowledge how it has hurt far too many people by looking the other way when confronted with the integrity of its leaders? Excuse me church, but your integrity is showing!

Having worked with powerful and talented people all of my life in the music business, athletics, government, education, and churches if I've made any mistake it's that I've been overly impressed by the position and power of people for a time and have forgotten that inside that person is an aching heart or an uncertainty or a problem that only God can solve. The truth is if you assume everyone really needs the Lord then you won't take people for granted. I've come to realize that the division in the mind of God isn't between the sacred arena and a secular arena; the division is between the light and the dark—and there's a darkened world in both the secular and in the sacred. There's darkness across the face of the earth, across the street and within the church and its leadership and the Lord wants to seed it all with the sons and daughters of light.

When your authority is based on the position or title and you need a position or title to lead, chances are you're not a real leader. Real leaders lead with influence and not through manipulation and real ones have the character and integrity necessary for the position and the title. A new type of leader is reflected not by the force of their personality but is based on what they do by laying down their lives that builds a bridge for what they're going to accomplish. This new type of leader, whether In the church, business or government, in education or the home leads from brokenness and weakness rather than personal charisma or the appearance of strength through deception. Personality has failed to take us where only personal integrity can lead.

Under the old paradigm of church, the measure of success is by growth, whether in numbers, finances, or real estate. What we find is bigger buildings and smaller people leading them. In the new paradigm we base our success on FOCUS: faith, obedience, commitment, unity and servant-hood. God is looking for leaders who walk with a limp; those who like Jacob fought or wrestled with God and surrendered unconditionally to Him. He is looking for us to reach our destiny like Daniel through dependence, discipline and desire for Him and only Him. He is after those who will fulfill His Godly purposes as they relationally learn from the disappointments and challenges of following him through good times and bad and not by fleecing the flock or mismanaging one's own integrity and the integrity of those who follow you.

A future leader is a good leader if he consecrates himself in covenant with God's promises. The future holds a vision for alternative forms of faith communities, ones that will be covenantal and not just charismatic. A leader who realizes this begins to work with the youth and children to prepare them for a different type of church and world than the one we live in now. To do this we must take on a "death theology" and apply it to our church leadership. Christ said, "if you hold on to your life, you lose it, if you lose it for My sake, you'll save it." He is saying through "death theology" that we need to build into our structure the truth that we do not want to stay alive forever, that we have no plan to keep ourselves alive. The truth is this is the sin of self preservation which seems to have the present leadership mentality that I must survive by any means necessary even at the expense of my character and integrity or that of those who trust and follow them.

We will not lead by living in our past. The pastor is now a bishop and serves a network of covenant churches and ministries. So our vision is to move from a temple to a cathedral conceptually building a bridge to fulfilled promises through the D.N.A. of Divine Truth, Nurturing Relationships, and Apostolic mission. How then should we as a fellowship of churches avoid compromising our integrity on the altar of convenience or compromise? Five things present themselves from the New Testament doctrine of the church and help with our covenantal and doctrinal integrity.

First, **meaningful or regenerate or refocused church membership must be regained**. Meaningful membership will counter the culture of consumerism and compromise that the church now faces. A congregation full of members who understand their roles will result in a well-balanced church with more than the usual twenty percent of the members doing eighty percent of the work. In order for our members to take membership seriously, biblical expectations must be understood. A proper theological understanding of God's promises and purposes will affect the DNA and FOCUS the way we see our part in the local church. Moreover, the successful maintenance of regenerate and refocused church membership allows congregational leadership to function properly.

Second, **our churches must regain and act on the proper understanding of baptism.** The God-given ordinance has fallen into anonymity. With overly liberal challenges questioning its importance, many younger pastors and church workers have not been properly equipped to defend the doctrine of baptism. A discussion must take place regarding the various elements of baptism: baptism must be of believers, baptism must be by immersion, baptism is the outward symbol of the inward change, baptism is the public profession of faith, baptism is the door to the local church, and baptism begins the covenant relationship among believers in a local congregation. Only those participating in this ceremonial act of commitment to Christ may be accepted into the membership of the local church. Thus, baptism properly understood protects the entrance to the church while church discipline protects the continued integrity of the church. Be saved and be baptized are not options.

Third, **our churches must understand and maintain the proper view of the Lord's Supper.** A proper view of the Lord's Supper understands the ordinance is meaningful and not merely a quarterly addendum at the end of a service. A correct understanding of the Lord's Supper is that it is a meaningful event for remembering the work of Christ on the cross, celebrating the fellowship and unity of the body, and anticipating the triumphant return of Christ. In addition, the Lord's Supper understood correctly cannot be separate from church discipline and the regenerate nature of the congregation.

Fourth, **our churches must regain the proper practice of church discipline that always seeks restoration.** Church discipline can easily be twisted as a legalistic hammer with which one may beat others over the head. Such misuses do not exemplify biblical church discipline, which intentionally confronts members in sin, seeking both individual restoration and the maintenance of a pure body. The loss of biblical church discipline has led many onlookers to say that the church is no different than the world. This should never be the case; by requiring regenerate membership reinforced by biblical church discipline, the church will look very different from the world.

Finally, **our churches must address emerging and seeker trends, pointing out certain challenges to our theological practice.** We must examine proper theological practice in light of the success these movements have achieved. While the local church needs a new measuring stick for success other than mere numbers, finances and real estate the conversion or transformation of human lives does indeed represent the mission of the church; while equipping the saints for the work of the ministry is still the calling of its leaders.

Daniel the 6th chapter is important to us as modern believers. It is here that we learn the secret of Daniel's success. Somehow he managed to survive and thrive in a spiritually hostile environment while maintaining his integrity. That point is a good place to begin, because we, as Christians, live in a world of spiritual hostility where the temptation to compromise our faith and destroy our integrity is with us every day in so many ways.

The world doesn't want its conscience pricked and doesn't reward those who dare to stand up for what they believe. In fact with success comes attack, judgment, and condemnation. In some places standing up for Christ means suffering and death. It means ostracism, ridicule, scorn, being left out and perhaps being passed over. It often leads to tension at home and on the job, making it hard to maintain your integrity without compromise.

The book of Daniel tells us how to live for God in a hostile environment. His example shows us that it can be done but not without discomfort. If you don't compromise, you are sure to come into trouble sooner or later. The story of Daniel and the lion's den reminds us that there is a spiritual battle raging all around us. The devil himself is like a roaring lion who would devour us if he could (1Peter 5:8).

Therefore, it should not surprise us if the devil has an army of supporters whose major call in life is to harass us, trick us, and trip us up if they can and cause us to compromise our integrity. You can tell a lot about a person by the quality of his enemies. T.D. Jakes also warns us that if you are the smartest person in the room then you are in the wrong room. Integrity demands that we grow in grace and in knowledge. Some of us are far too comfortable being in a dumbed down environment where integrity counts for nothing.

Daniel must have been a good man because he had the right kind of enemies. The people who hated him were no friends of God. They came after his faith because they could find no fault in him, and they had no answer for what he believed. Make no mistake, your integrity is showing to both your friends and your enemies.

The only question is when the time comes will your integrity withstand the people around you?

FOCUS

"Entering the Promise Dimension"

In Genesis 35:1-3, "God said to Jacob (also known as Israel) Get ready and move to Bethel and settle there. Build an altar there to the God who appeared to you when you fled from your brother Esau. So Jacob told everyone in his household, get rid of all your pagan idols, purify yourself, and put on clean clothing. We are now going to Bethel, where I will build an altar to the God who answered my prayers when I was in distress. He has been with me wherever I have gone."

We must see God's promise, and then we must embrace the idea of the promise, before we can agree with God in our spirit to see it come to pass. We all know of the promises of the bible, from Abraham and Isaac, of Israel and the Promised Land and finally the promise of salvation and the coming of our Savior Jesus Christ. In each of these promises, they were aware of the promise, and then they had to stand firm and embrace the idea coming to the place of agreement to see it come to pass.

God puts promises in our hearts and those promises are ones He desire's to fulfill. Maybe like me, you have been waiting for the Lord to fulfill a promise. Others of you may feel that you don't have any promises, which is okay for you. But for those of us whose hearts are being stirred because there is something great being birthed in you, allow the Lord to show you what it is, then stand firm and embrace the promise and agree with the Lord's timing and see that promise fulfilled. You see God has been with us all this time. Now we are about to move into a new dimension of his promise. We are about to realize the fulfillment of the goodness of His promise in our lives and ministry.

Potential's ability to realize goodness depends on the interplay between free will and the circumstances that create the environment for its expression. If the environment encourages goodness, potential is blessed; if the environment does not encourage goodness, or worse, discourages goodness, through intimidation, bitterness, distress, doubt or disobedience potential is severely handicapped. It is doubtful whether under such circumstances potential will ever realize the fullness of its expression to accomplish goodness. Thus, a negative environment hinders the promises of God; making the fulfillment of those promises difficult to be experienced or expressed in your life.

We have spent time preparing to "Sit at the Table of the Lord's Favor" and we have truly been realizing the blessings of the Lord as we have been captured, captivated, consecrated and dedicated for the Master's use and blessed with favor in the land of the living, for myself personally and our ministry vision corporately.

When we talk about being blessed or receiving blessings we must remember that "Blessing" means to encourage and empower potential to become reality. Blessing is the use of potential to do good things – meaning, to serve God. Likewise, "To Curse" means to hinder potential so that it never becomes a reality. Curses do not allow potential to accomplish goodness - meaning, they do not allow potential for use in the service of God.

Over the course of the last two years we have been like the people of Israel when they came to the place called Shechem. Starting with Abraham's entry into the land of Canaan and ending with the Jewish nation's entry into Canaan (at the ceremony of blessings and curses between the mountains of Gerizim and Ebal); the Jewish people were asked to choose. They were to proclaim how they would use the gift of the land or the potential of its goodness as they reached this dimension of promise. Would they use its potential and their own in an integrated and concerted effort to synergistically accomplish God's intent and purpose for placing them in the Promised land; or, would they squander the gift of the land, its potential and their own, in pursuing other agenda's removed and therefore in opposition to God's wishes?

The job of each believer of God's promises, and thus our job is to study God's manifest actions and emulate them to the best of our comprehension and ability; to enjoy God's grace, extend God's glory and establish God's throne or authority in our lives. In doing so, we express our absolute faith in God that "make God's will our own so that God will make our will His." So long as we do as God wants God does as we want. The reality is that if we make His will our own then automatically we are in concert with God's will entering as a result the promise dimension and thus can have His promises fulfilled in our lives. The only thing we should want is what God wants. There is no conflict or contradiction between our wants and desires and God's wishes and commands.

The children of Israel understood that their being in the land of Promise could mean success or failure and they had to be clear as to their intentions. If their intentions were to serve God and enjoy the grace, extend the glory and establish the Throne or authority of God they would be successful; if not, the land would deny their attempts at settling and cultivating it. The Land or what I call "The Promise Dimension" would chase them away.

As we arrive at this new "Promise Dimension" of God's purpose for our lives and ministry our actions will bless or curse our arrival at the new level and the opportunity and fulfillment of potential blessings as promised by God's calling us to come into Holy Covenant with Him as His Cathedral of Faith.

This basic concept of the symbiotic relationship between the people of God and the land or dimension of promise is not new. From the very beginning of time the relationship between human behavior and the availability of potential blessings is clear. Adam and Eve had a perfect world that took care of them. Their access to the Garden of Eden left them free to focus solely on understanding God and His intentions for humanity. Their focus was to be on enjoying the grace, extending the glory and establishing the Throne (dominion or authority of God). Once they sinned, Adam and Eve's disobedience caused God to chase them out of the Garden of Eden and the struggle for realizing the fulfillment of God's promises began. To the extent that they listened to God and was obedient was the extent to which the dimension of God's promises gave them the fullness of its bounty.

As we move from a Temple to a Cathedral, we will find our potential is in the faithfulness of the families that covenant with us to fulfill the potential of the new dimension of opportunity and promise. Thus, blessing and curses begin at the door of each family that makes up the Cathedral. The responsibility of the parents then is to position themselves and their children to line up with the purpose, plan and promises of God through their faithful obedience as good stewards of every good and perfect gift of God. Parents are like the binding and cover of a book with the pages being the children. When the binding begins to fray and the covers fall off, the pages are in danger of separating.

The truth is that as we add pages to the family book there comes a time when the covers and binding are not strong enough to hold all the pages in place. Eventually new books are be bound. If each page is a person and each book a family, then the CATHEDRAL is the library. Clearly, the rules for organizing a library are far more involved and complex than the organization of a page or book. As we realize the fulfillment of the Promise Dimension we fill the Cathedral like a library with the blessings of the Lord and with the stories of each of our lives as we enjoy the grace, extend the glory and establish the throne with our potential.

On his deathbed, Israel feared for the cohesiveness of his children. His concern was not as much for the twelve sons who were the progenitors of the nation as it was for the endless generations yet to be born. How could he aid them in maintaining familial connections during the difficult years ahead of them? How could he help them become a nation?

For many years Jacob had been lingering some thirty miles away from Bethel and had paid dearly for his disobedience. Bethel means "the house of God." So he, like some of us, disobediently stayed out of the house of God or just beyond a faithful focus for much too long. When will you make yourself available to come faithfully into the Promise Dimension and join us as we move from what we've been to what God has promised we can become? For many years many of you have been lingering just beyond your promise as individuals and as a family and collectively as a part of the families of faith; and some of you have paid the cost for your disobedience dearly. You have declared your faith in the vision of the fellowship, made commitments to be obedient, pledged your unity and service but lingered just outside of a faithful fulfillment of your promise for years.

I call on you to "RENEW your FOCUS to enter the PROMISE DIMENSION." Declare your commitment to your potential, your promise and that of your families by rebuilding the altar of your commitment, get rid of your pagan idols and the false gods who have been keeping you in distress, disobedience, doubt and debt. Make plans to come forth and face the Giant of the Spirit of Intimidation hindering your purpose, promise and God's plan for your life. Purify yourselves as many are now doing through rebaptism, renewal of marriage vows, and refocus of their commitments and calling, and putting on clean clothes.

In the Scriptures, washing the body and changing clothes symbolizes making a NEW BEGINNING or coming into the PROMISE DIMENSION. Like dirt, sin or separation from God and his promises, is defiling and must be washed away according to Psalm 51:2-4: "Wash me thoroughly of my iniquity, and cleanse me from my sin. For I acknowledge my transgressions and my sin is always before me. Against You, You only, have I sinned, and done this evil in your sight; that I may be found just when you speak, and blameless when you judge."

The Lord begins to speak to Jacob and told him to move to Bethel, the House of God and settle down there. Jacob already knew that Bethel was God's appointed place for him and his family (Genesis 31:13) but he like so many of us was slow to obey. Has God told you to come back to the house of God this season? Maybe it is because He doesn't want you to miss His Promise Dimension due to your continued disobedience.

Many of the problems in our Christian lives and in the local churches, we so unfaithfully attend and support, result from incomplete obedience. We know what the Lord wants us to do, we start to do it, and then we stop. When we don't continue to obey God and accomplish his will, even what we've done starts to . . . die! What Jesus said to the church in Sardis, beloved he now is saying to us, "Wake up! Strengthen what little remains, for even what is left is almost dead." I find that your actions do not meet the requirements of my God" (Revelation 3:2).

So like Jacob, I am calling for a time of cleansing for everybody and the first thing we have to do is to get rid of stuff we have made idols and have begun to worship instead of Almighty God. Jacob discovered that his wife Rachel had stolen her father's household idols (Genesis 31:19). Instead of facing Laban, and trusting the Lord to keep his promises and work things out, Jacob became intimated by it all and instead fled with his family like a criminal escaping justice. This was an act of fear and unbelief; which is a stubborn unwillingness to obey and trust in the Lord, and lean not to his own understanding. This was not an act of faith, as so many of us attempt to believe about ourselves as we slip away from the church and the obedience to God and his purposes like thieves in the night leaving the rest of us to fulfill the promises and the responsibilities we all say we are committed to.

Jacob repented and later admitted to his uncle Laban that he in fact had departed secretly and quickly because he was afraid, he was intimidated (Genesis 31:31). Beloved, it isn't enough to know and do the will of God; we must also do His will (watch this now) IN THE WAY HE WANTS IT DONE! IN THE WAY THAT WILL GLORIFY HIM THE MOST. When you leave the church like a thief, stop paying your tithe or supporting your commitments in ministry, giving or serving, act dishonestly in leading others to become unfaithful along with you, and like Rachel taking and hiding her father's household idols, you leave God little choice but to withhold his promises and eventually come and wrestle with you and your choices to disobey Him. Confronted by an angry Laban, Jacob had little choice but to come clean.

My question is what is intimidating you and keeping you from coming clean? What household idol have you hidden in your heart and decided it was worth it to hide from God and the church? What made you run away from the PROMISE DIMENSION? Was it impatience, petulance, impurity, pettiness, pouting, putting on a front, pleasing someone else?

Here is the secret testimony of faith in the promise dimension. Life isn't easy, but if we submit to God's disciplines and let him guide us in our decisions, we can endure the difficulties triumphantly and develop the kind of character that enjoys God's grace, extends God's glory, and establishes God's throne in the earth. We can conquer by claiming promises like I Peter 5:10: "In his kindness God called you to share in his eternal glory by means of Christ Jesus. So after you have suffered a little while, he will restore, support, and strengthen you, and he will place you on a firm foundation."

The God of Jacob never fails. God knows what he is doing and what his purpose is for us. He is in complete control no matter how difficult the fiery trials and the storms of life may become.

The most important quality of the Promise Dimension is humility. Humility, to put the record straight, has nothing to do with weakness. When we humble ourselves and admit our mistakes and offer a humble spirit before God we operate from a position and posture of strength the world doesn't know nor can promote. We know God loves us; and he calls us to the love of others. We also know that God loves other people and are therefore objects of our concern. When one becomes a leader as you and I have, then it is simply to lead people to God and to share His love with them. I Corinthians 10:21 declares, "You cannot drink from the cup of the Lord and the cup of demons too; you cannot have a part in both the Lord's Table and the table of demons." Why continue to halt thee between two different and competing opinions. Either have faith in God or in your Baal gods, idols or opinions and demonic associations. You cannot enter the promise dimension like a thief in the night or by drinking from the cup of demons and their deceptions.

We must be consistent in the choices we make. If not, we become unstable and easily persuaded to change sides in accordance with the circumstances that we are experiencing. The church of God must be humble, cohesive and comprehensive; in other words unified, interconnected, solid and not wishy-washy, faithful and interrelated. Ephesians 4:14-15 says, "Then we will no longer be infants, tossed back and forth by the waves, and blown here and there by every wind of teaching and by the cunning and craftiness of men in their deceitful scheming. Instead, speaking the truth in love, we will in all things grow up into Him".

The Sincere church in the promise dimension must cohere so that it presents a formidable argument against the lies of a counterfeit. Paul urged the Philippians in the promise dimension that the way to present a formidable argument against any enemy was to be careful how they conducted themselves in everyday life.

"Only be sure as citizens [of the kingdom . . . THE PROMISE DIMENSION] so to conduct yourselves {that} your manner of life {will be} worthy of the good news [the Gospel] of Christ, so that whether I [do] come and see you or am absent, I may hear this of you; that you are standing firm in united spirit and purpose, striving side by side and contending with a single mind for the faith of the glad tidings (the Gospel)" Philippians 1:27.

As people of faith we always have hope in the PROMISE DIMENSION.

FOCUS

A Covenant of Trust

Anointing gives you the ability to say things with boldness. It allows you to say things that really are true without regret, and pull the covers off of the deceptions of people and their ability to hide and influence others with their deception. When you have this boldness it causes people to get thirsty or flee. It sometimes results in your boldness and covenant of trust in your being offended by the responses of people you commit your life to. When people offend you with this anointing, you can find that offenses can become your best friend. Offenses can be good if it makes you hungry and willing to take criticisms and grow from them. You can use what we see as offenses as a way to change your thinking and let your life go to new levels.

Because we have little use for authority in this generation we don't appreciate when someone talks to us authoritatively so we get offended. We now live in a fatherless generation where the only voice of authority is mommas. When young men especially, get to the work place, or the school, or the church and hear an authoritative male voice and that man has to come down on them they often can't take it and quit on school, work, or faith. It is because they are not use to the sound of authority coming from that voice.

So if our youth can't do what they want to do and have not heard the voice of authority coming from a male they quickly get offended and can't understand why their male boss has scheduled them to work and they can't get off on Friday night to go to the party with their friends so they quit. When they come to church and the pastor tells them they need to pull their pants up or they can't sleep in the pew or they need to get rest at home by turning off the television earlier or getting off the Facebook social network and stop using it for inappropriate communication with friends then they turn off the voice of authority and become offended.

We are a generation of quitters. We quit on responsibilities. We quit on marriages whether we are in or out of the church. We quit on ministries. We walk away from the responsibilities to our children and families. We leave assignments undone without regrets or regard for their implications. We quit on each other and ultimately we quit on God!

Stories of fallen leaders are not hard to find. Many accounts focus on sexual misconduct and irresponsible behavior; but other kinds of misconduct are well represented as well, including the misappropriation of funds and the misuse of authority and power. That these stories come to our attention through the media and other channels so regularly that we are more saddened than shocked by them bears witness to the critical nature of this problem. The misconduct of those in authority whether in the government, the school, business, the home or in the church is a crisis which demands immediate attention and threatens our covenant of trust with people who depend on it for their growth, development, salvation and focus.

Facing this present reality should not make us long for an innocent past when "these things just didn't happen." The truth of the matter is the history of the church serves as a poignant reminder that "these things" have always happened. The task before us is both critical and urgent, but at the same time perennial. Christian ethics and authentic discipleship is the critical and urgent task for all

Christians of every age and is the responsibility of every generation to become good stewards of. We must come together with a covenant of trust to use our anointing and authority to pray, plan, purpose, prepare and present principles and polices as we partner for fulfilled promises. Christians who embrace "the priesthood of all believers" are doubly reminded of this truth. Since we believe that all Christians have a calling to minister, becoming the leaders they are looking for, we must also affirm that following Jesus does not mean one thing for those called to the vocation of ministry and something less for laity leaders, volunteers, parents, educators and lawmakers. We should not expect one level of discipleship and ethical behavior for pastors and other professional ministers, politicians and educational professionals and another level for church members, homemakers, parents and volunteers or those whose ministries are lived out day to day in homes, work places and excursions to the mall. The high calling, which is ours in Christ Jesus, is just that—ours; the responsibility and privilege of a covenant of grace for the whole Body of Christ is to serve God and God's creation in trusted covenant and sincere focused Christian ministry.

I know this sounds a little bold but that is what anointing does it gives you the boldness to do or say that which you could never do or say in and of your self. All of us have sinned and fall short of the Glory of God so who am I to point out these things so boldly? But the truth is still the truth even when it offends you. What you need to do is get your offense out of the way and deal with the truth it has revealed about you. Here is the question: How do you deal with an authoritative voice in your life, in your house, or in the church? When you hear it, do you get offended, upset, and turn it off and just quit or respect it and humbly honor it with your response? Do you have a covenant of trust with the LORD and an authority figure in your life? Someone that holds you accountable and who themselves take seriously their leadership role in your life, ministry and destiny?

Then, there is the issue of those who have this authority and how they use it. Do we use this authority to lord over and misuse our power for selfish reasons? The truth is God gives you this authority as a "Covenant of Trust" not to be taken lightly. God never lets your boss or even your pastor control your destiny. He only gives them a covenant of trust for use as stewards in helping Him to fulfill His plans for your life. We are at best as pastors, parents and community, family and church partners, just stewards of the promises of God.

Authority is not size, or talent, or even your office. Authority is respect, honor and the weight of God's Glory in covenant trust with its use, availability to its user and the responsibility for how it is used to guide lives and promises. The truth of the matter is that we have got to learn how to listen to another sound in order for God to change you.

For a lot of us we have never had anyone speak to us boldly. Because of the primarily female headed single parent households and lack of men sharing the responsibility of authority in our churches we now see women as the main voice of authority in the lives of this generation. We fail to appreciate the differences in the approaches and natures of the genders. The female voice is primarily a voice of comfort. A woman in and of herself is a sedative. This generation is so comfortable being raised by mothers that when a voice of power comes into the life of this generation in the form of male authority it is a strange sound. The male voice, instead of being a sedative, becomes a strong stimulant and its power is abusive when used incorrectly or without integrity.

The covenant of trust calls for us to move a poverty mindset generation into a kingdom authorized fulfillment of promises for people chosen by God: captured, consecrated, and dedicated for the Master's use. We must be consecrated as vessels of grace in order to be invited to the table of His favor and fulfill our promise as his stewards.

But we must also keep in mind that the enemy desires for each of us to end up in the valley of despair instead. Neither being broke or broken is fun. Money problems are not fun. Joblessness is not fun. Indebtedness and lack is not fun. Relationship problems are not fun. Unfulfilled promises can be challenging, devastating and destructive to a poverty mind set generation and causes the abandonment of FOCUS (faith, obedience, commitment, unity and servant-hood) as we become slaves to doubt, debt, and dysfunction. Poor stewardship of our integrity is the main culprit of our corporate pain in the church, homes and community.

As we argue over finances and faith and whether we will use our available resources to go to work or worship is not fun. Though it is not fun it is too much of a reality in the lives of people and the promises of God for our lives and churches, homes and communities we serve. When God gives you a voice to influence the most vulnerable of his people, the left out, left over and often left behind of the community not yet visited, it is given with a covenant of trust. The one with responsibility of using this authority gets beat up a lot. Using this authority with integrity, intensity and influence on the lives God has given them is for the fulfillment of God's promises and stewardship of His purposes for His church and people.

Because you speak to vulnerable people, there are those who question you and what you have because you speak to vulnerable people. Where you live, or what you drive and wear becomes a distraction to people because you can't be fulfilling promises, according to them, if you yourself are benefiting in the anointing on your life. The covenant of trust is a protective mechanism for the lost, left out and left behind; and for the authority we've been given to be stewards of God's promises. If you are in poverty of soul, sin sick and lost in the world wind of dysfunction we are committed to using our authority and our Focus to lift you and your families so you can realize the fulfillment of God's promises in your life.

We are here to break the bondage of spiritual doubt, debt and dysfunction of soul that permeates this generation's thinking, behavior and faith, so each of us may enjoy the grace, extend the glory and establish the throne of God's authority in our hearts, heads hands and feet. Walking out our faith with dependence, desire and discipline as a covenant of trust is our committed focus.

The covenant of trust is our commitment to God to speak boldly to the negative mindsets and dysfunction taking over this generation's ability to fulfill God's promises for their lives. The lack of this commitment keeps us locked where we are and unable to move into the places of promise God has called us to. No matter what you cannot shout your way out of bad habits and unfaithful decision making negatively affecting your life. Though the truth is that we are some of the most generous people it is not always our hearts that is the problem but our heads. We have not captured the mindset of the kingdom and the focus of covenant promise that the wealth of the wicked is being laid up for the righteous. In other words the fulfillment of God's promises in the lives of the people with a covenant of trust puts us in position for that transfer as we become faithful stewards of a kingdom focused lifestyle.

In the Book of Acts, Jesus has now died and gone back to heaven having fulfilled the covenant of trust through His death, burial and resurrection. The covenant of trust is now transferred to the twelve disciples who are now the twelve apostles and stewards of this trust. The Book of Acts is the acts of these apostles or the acts of the Holy Spirit in their lives giving them authority through the covenant of trust to fulfill God's promises in the lives of his people who make up his church.

Matthew, Mark, Luke and John were the acts of Jesus. Now here in the book of Acts, Jesus has transferred the covenant of trust upon the stewardship of the twelve and the Book chronicles what they did with it. With their covenant they built a bridge network impacting the whole known world under the anointing Jesus imparted to them.

In Acts 16:16-20 look what happens to the Apostle Paul, who I might add, is not one of the original twelve. "One day as we were going down to the place of prayer, we met a demon-possessed slave girl. She was a fortune-teller who earned a lot of money for her masters. She followed Paul and the rest of us, shouting, 'these men are servants of the Most High God, and they have come to tell you how to be saved."

Look at this with me. It says she was a slave possessed with a demon. She is outwardly and inwardly bound. In other words, she was in total bondage. It was a physical, emotional, and spiritual enslavement. Enslaved physically to the demands of somebody else or some authority with no covenant of trust; enslaved emotionally and in her decision making to the will of a demon. Let's just say this is a picture of the jacked-up situation many of us find ourselves in as we confront this generation.

This spirit she had enabled her to foretell the future. So people would go to her before they would place their bets or buy their lotto tickets. This spirit working through her would give them information on the future then they would bet and profit from her information. She was working for the profit of others, while they were stewards over her demon guided lifestyle for their own benefit. This reminds me that churches with unscrupulous leaders have profited from demon possessed women (in debt, doubt and depression) whose only covenant was with untrustworthy pastors, husbands and even sister friends. They were using their weaknesses, fears, frustrations and trust against them while taking no responsibility for generations of unhappy, unsatisfied and unfaithful lives of woman and their children.

The bible goes on to say, "this went on day after day until Paul got so exasperated that he turned and said to the demon within her, 'I command you in the name of Jesus Christ to come out of her" and instantly it left her."

This girl was trying like so many of us to do something that looked spiritual but has an undercurrent of distraction instead of a dedicated covenant of trust. We understand that in this season of consecration on our way to fulfilled promises there will be people among us who look spiritual but have no covenant of trust and are only there as demon stewards to divide and distract. They call it sharing with you a prayer request, calling you for support, and touching and agreeing with you as your life becomes a wreck and their false witness becomes but the undercurrent that takes you away from trusting God and who He has sent as an authoritative voice for your life. They come around like vipers in the garden of your promise to engage you in gossip, complaints, and offensive discoveries and discussions that jack your swagga, steal your promise and cause you to miss your blessing. They steward demonic dialogue through cell phones, text messages, Face Book and Twitter causing pain and bondage to sin, suffering and selfish behavior.

The bible goes on to say, 'Her master's hopes of wealth were now shattered, so they grabbed Paul and Silas and dragged them before the authorities at the marketplace. The whole city is in an uproar because of these Jews! They shouted to the city officials "They are teaching customs that are illegal for us Romans to practice." They are using their authority to change the nature of church and confronting powerfully that which is holding individuals, families, communities and churches in bondage to the ineffectiveness of traditions long past their usefulness and the lack of Focus by leaders entrusted with the stewardship of the covenant of grace.

The bible further states "A mob quickly formed against Paul and Silas and the city officials ordered them stripped and beaten with wooden rods. They were severely beaten, and thrown into prison. The jailer (the industrial prison complex) was ordered to make sure they didn't escape. So the jailer put them into the inner dungeon and clamped their feet in the stocks."

All they did was set the girl free! They were using their authority boldly and their covenant of trust faithfully. Now everybody is upset. Why aren't people celebrating their commitment? Why aren't they praising God and enjoying the grace, extending the glory and establishing the throne?

The girl is possessed and it is ugly and takes her will away. Nobody in the city or the church it seems is bothered by how she is living. They just continue to take advantage of her, profiting from her pain. Her life is devastated and she is enslaved to the will and purposes of a demon and the negative control of those who profit from her dilemma. She has no will or life of her own. All she has are people in her life that don't want her to get better or be free.

The Apostle Paul, with the authority of boldness and just a word cast the demon out. Everybody should have been glorifying and praising God. Instead the people are mad, and they take hold of the ones who in the covenant of trust used the boldness of God given authority to set her free. They take them before the city officials; have them beaten with rods of wood, locked up and their feet bound with locks and chains. Whenever someone in covenant with God has the audacity to set the captive free and break the bondage of demon possessed lives it seems the religious, the uncommitted crowd and the men and women in the lives of the captive get together to beat up on the one responsible for their freedom.

They did all this when they saw that their means of profit was gone! It is amazing what people will do for a dollar and some unauthorized control and power. It was in the best interest of the people who profited to keep the girl weak. When not having many resources, or people with integrity as authorities in your life, has you tormented by debt, doubts and depressed and being possessed by the demons of dysfunction there is a certain group of people you should be aware of that it is in their best interest for you to remain that way.

It is time for you to make a focused commitment to a covenant of trust and begin to stand up for people who stand up for you; and stop letting people who profit from your painfully produced anointing to beat you down as leaders and stewards of the promise. Your weakness, whatever it is, you can believe that somebody is profiting from it. While God has sent someone to be an authoritative steward of your promise with a covenant of trust through his grace and power.

When you review this 16th chapter of Acts we can see that the work of the covenant of trust in the LORD progresses through difficulties and challenges. Sometimes the workers have problems with each other, and then sometimes the problems come from people outside of our covenant of trust.

Instead of complaining or calling on God and other people to judge one another maybe we ought to begin like these two men, Paul and Silas to pray, plan, purpose, use Godly principles, partnership and commit to fulfilling our promise so that everyone in our households and in the house of God can rejoice because we all believe in God and in his covenant of trust!

What is the covenant of trust? Godly ethics begins with integrity, defined as "completeness" or "wholeness." Jesus captures the gospel sense of integrity with the command, "Be perfect as your heavenly Father is perfect" (Matt. 5:48). In the English text "perfect" renders the Greek word teleios which means "complete." So it begins with a pursuit of the mystery of perfection or completeness. People who are broken themselves cannot sincerely steward a covenant of trust. Broken people break people.

Jesus' teaching concludes with his authoritative interpretation of the Law ("You have heard that it was said. . . . But I say to you") which in turn interprets the Sermon's theme, "unless your righteousness exceeds that of the scribes and Pharisees, you will never enter the kingdom of heaven" (Matt. 5:20). Integrity in the covenant of trust entails being completed or formed by the Word of God which comes to us in Jesus Christ. Jesus' conclusion to the Sermon suggests that such integrity is the embodiment of wisdom. Listen to what He says: "Everyone then who hears these words of mine and acts on them will be like a wise man who built his house on rock. The rain fell, the floods came, and the winds blew and beat on that house, but it did not fall, because it had been founded on rock. And everyone who hears these words of mine and does not act on them will be like a foolish man who built his house on sand. The rain fell, and the floods came, and the winds blew and beat against that house, and it fell—and great was its fall! (Matt. 5:24-27)

The reaction of those who heard the Sermon connects integrity to the life-changing impact of the covenant of trust as heard through the boldness of the gospel of truth: "Now when Jesus had finished saying these things, the crowds were astounded at his teaching, for he taught them as one having authority, and not as their scribes" (Matt. 5:28-29).

We begin to have integrity in the covenant of trust in the gospel sense when we hear and follow Jesus on our way to becoming a truthful people. Receiving, embodying, and telling the truth of God in Christ is the essence of integrity. Indeed, the failure of ministerial integrity is in large measure the failure to know and bear witness to this very truth. We cannot be stewards of the demonic purposes of this generation and in covenant trust with God's purposes, promises and plans for our generation without the power of integrity.

The church is complicit in the loss of integrity in the church, in the home, and in the community. We live in a consumer society, and churches routinely function as subsets of this society. We come to church as individuals with needs, and we expect those in authority to meet our needs. We feel guilty, and we need forgiveness. We feel lonely, and we need companionship. We feel grief, and we need to be comforted. We feel depressed, hopeless, empty, alienated, trapped, aimless, and we need encouragement, assurance, reconciliation, liberation, and direction just like the woman in Acts 16. The last thing we need to find in church are those who are not good stewards of their authority and our trust.

We feel bored, and we need to be entertained. Sensitive to our needs, ministries and churches try to meet them, offering friendship, understanding, motivation, and spiritual inspiration instead of the truth. While people's needs are heart-felt, and ministry leader's attempts to meet them are genuine, the consumer approach to church and ministry undermines ministerial integrity, and the covenant of trust. Christian ministry is not first and foremost about identifying and meeting the needs of people, but about leading people to follow Jesus and thus to become the people of God committed to and focused on a covenant of trust in his promises, plan and purpose for our lives.

Following Jesus, we are called to be the salt of the earth and the light of the world, to love our enemies, to be agents of reconciliation, to do justice for "the least of these," the left out, left over and left behind of the community not yet visited; to love God as we love one another, to serve God as we serve one another, and to bear witness to enjoy the grace, extend the glory and establish the throne and the reality that "the Word became flesh and lived among us . . . full of grace and truth" (John 1:14).

When the task of ministry becomes defined by something less than helping the people of God to be formed by the covenant of grace and trust as defined by the way of Jesus, our responsibility to ministerial integrity completeness is bound to suffer. This is not to deny the clear connection between human needs and Christian ministry, but rather to give an account of what it means to lose (and to regain) ministerial and familial integrity as stewards of the promise with a covenant of trust.

Life in the Body of Christ inevitably raises power issues, and these issues are central to ministerial ethics and the covenant of trust. An important scriptural starting point for interpreting power in the community of faith is Philippians 2:1-11: "If then there is any encouragement in Christ, any consolation from love, any sharing in the Spirit, any compassion and sympathy, make my joy complete: be of the same mind, having the same love, being in full accord and of one mind. Do nothing from selfish ambition or conceit, but in humility regard others as better than you. Let each of you look not to your own interests, but to the interests of others. Let the same mind be in you that was in Christ Jesus, who, though he was in the form of God, did not regard equality with God as something to be exploited, but emptied himself, taking the form of a slave, being born in human likeness. And being found in human form, he humbled himself and became obedient to the point of death— even death on a cross. Therefore God also highly exalted him and gave him the name that is above every name, so that at the name of Jesus every knee should bend, in heaven and on earth and under the earth, and every tongue should confess that Jesus Christ is Lord, to the glory of God the Father."

The faithfulness of this teaching is always critical to congregational life, just as its disregard accounts for many of the saddest moments in church history. The call to Focus (faith, obedience, commitment, unity and servant-hood) is the high calling of Christ's ministers, paid or unpaid, vocational or volunteer.

In Matthew and parallel passages in Mark and Luke, Jesus said we should not "lord it over" one another and that the greatest of God's people must be servants rather than tyrants (Matt. 20:20-28). Jesus' instruction to his disciples suggests that the corporate executive model of the pastorate in which the pastor rules the church fails to appreciate this distinctively Christian sense of leadership. Christian leaders lead by serving. Power, in the conventional sense, is in effect turned on its head, so that the greatness of leadership is not determined by how many lives we control, but by how faithfully we serve each life with whom God has entrusted us.

To confirm this point and to mute our every attempt to revise the meaning of service, Jesus concludes this instruction with the sentence, "whoever wishes to be first among you must be your slave" (Matt. 20:27). "Slave" is descriptively clear here as so devastatingly painful in Acts 16 with the demon girl. Ministers cannot honestly claim to serve congregations by overpowering them. According to the gospel, the faithful stewardship of power in congregational life paradoxically entails the renunciation of power. This revolutionary subordination is ethically normative for the people of God and stands in judgment over the misuse of power in the community of faith.

When ministers attempt to create churches in their own image, consider the church's property as their own property, access the church treasury as their own treasury, manipulate church members and church life on behalf of their own self-interests, they violate the Christian stewardship of power and the covenant of trust.

Positively, Paul exemplifies the meaning of servanthood in ministry as honoring every member of the Body of Christ. Just as the human body consists of many members and thrives on their comprehensive interworking, so the Body of Christ depends on the collaboration of the diverse spiritual gifts of church members. 1 Corinthians 12:23 presses the implication of a crucial part of Paul's analogy ("those members of the body we think less honorable we clothe with greater honor") to mean that we particularly honor the contributions of church members who in conventional thinking might not seem very important. Again, the left out, left over, and left behind of the community not yet visited. The bold confronting of the demon possessed with doubt, debt and dysfunctional attitudes. The servant approach to power is unconventional precisely in that it reverses the slope of conventional social stratification, assuming the vantage point of "below" rather than "above." Instead of people on top wielding exclusive authority, people on the bottom have authority and significance as well through a covenant of trust.

In very close context with the call to servant-hood in the gospel passages quoted above are other teachings which have implications regarding the stewardship of power. In Matthew 18:15, Jesus instructs his disciples, if another member of the church sins against you, go and point out the fault when the two of you are alone. If the member listens to you, you have regained that one. Jesus goes on to say that if the offender refuses the reconciling initiative, the one who has been offended should continue to make reconciling initiatives until the offender "refuses to listen even to the church." At that point, the offender should become "as a Gentile and tax collector," that is, the subject of the church's missionary activity. Jesus concludes his instruction with a remarkable statement, "Truly I tell you, whatever you bind on earth will be bound in heaven, and whatever you loose on earth will be loosed in heaven" (Matt. 18:18).

Two implications regarding the stewardship of power in Matthew 18:15-20 complement the call to servant-hood and the covenant of trust. First, ministry involves us in reconciling initiatives which many of us would consider risky. Issues (offenses) should not be swept under the rug and forgotten, but faced positively and redemptively. Jesus describes these initiatives as persistent, concluding in the possible removal of the offender from church membership. Second, the followers of Jesus are invested with the authority to bind or loose, i.e., to hold onto or release offenses, "for where two or three are gathered in my name, I am there among them" (Matt. 18:20).

The term "offense" is not defined or qualified and could presumably include moral transgressions as well as personal attacks. The same Jesus, who in the context of Matthew's gospel issues several calls to servant-hood, here instructs his followers to take reconciling initiatives, to be persistent in doing so, and then grants them power to bind and to loose. Clearly, servant ministry requires courageous leadership.

We tend to avoid the kinds of initiatives prescribed by Jesus exactly because they are risky, bold, and authoritative and may lead to confrontations. But the one who calls us to servant ministry and a covenant of trust and power calls us also to congregational leadership, to be good stewards of the very power we possess as ministry leaders, which is the power to claim and reclaim lives in Jesus' name. The sort of leadership and exercise of power prescribed here is not imperial, but distinctively Christian and consistent with the way of the cross and the kingdom of God and his Christ. This is not the power of the tyrant who threatens, extorts, and demonically manipulates and unfaithfully profits, but the power of the good shepherd who simply will not give up on lost sheep. To be faithful to Jesus' call to servant ministry is to be willing to be good stewards of the power resident in spiritual leadership.

The way of Jesus is the way of the cross, which is not only the center of salvation but also the ethical norm of our common life of integrity. Jesus takes up the cross and commands his followers to do likewise. Paul's application of this central truth to the Body of Christ is that we should become servants of one another as Christ has served us.

As the body of Christ we are in a covenant of trust with Christ and one another.

FOCUS

Choices You Make, Chances You Take!

Life is about choices. Life is truly choice driven. Life is full of choices; choices that affect us on an everyday basis in everything we do which means our everyday choices are not without significance. Our choices affect us and others in dramatic ways whether we see it immediately or not. So much so that when you make bad choices there is no need for a devil to be in your life. Your bad choices affect your life negatively enough to alter your life and not in a good way. When you make a bad decision there is no need for demons. What your bad decisions accomplish no demon could do any better. There are some people we never should have dealt with in the first place, so it was not an attack of the devil but the choice you made to deal with the wrong person that messed up your life.

Some people want to claim demonic attacks on their life when the truth is it is their bad choices in choosing people to be in relationship with. Have you ever considered that the person wasn't your kind, wasn't like you - born again? They were not in God's plan for you; not going where you were going and have nothing in common with the purpose for your life. While still others claim the devil has attacked their finances, when could it be that you have mismanaged your finances, buying unnecessary things before you paid your tithes, paid your bills and paid yourself?

Sadly, when people come to the end of their life, they leave their families to foot the bill for their funeral. But it is not the devil it was you not purchasing life insurance. Instead you were drinking at happy hour, or playing blackjack at the casino or buying that extra pair of shoes you were only going to wear one time. Spending what it would have cost you in paying the premium, you become a burden in death to your family.

You make choices today that will open doors to your tomorrow. If you don't like where you find yourself today it is probably because a bad choice got you there. What is so awesome about life in Christ is that you don't have to stay in the life of bad decisions. God will teach what you need to change today, in order to make tomorrow look different. In the Bible, this is the Law of Sowing and Reaping. Galatians 6:7-8 says, "Do not be deceived, God is not mocked; for whatever a man sows, this he will also reap. For the one who sows to his own flesh shall from the flesh reap corruption, but the one who sows to the Spirit shall from the Spirit reap eternal life." I like to call this "Choices you Make Chances you Take!"

An African proverb says, "If you want to know the end of a thing first look at its beginning." A boundary is your personal "property line." It defines who you are, where you end, and where others begin. When we know what we want and do not want, what we are for and against, what we love and hate, what is for me" and what is "not me," we are setting boundaries. Far too many people do not set boundaries for their choices in life; therefore, without them the lines are a blur and as a result it affects other people.

I have learned that God will take me through a process that leads to a moment. Some people, especially church people want the moments and not the process. The truth is that we go through a whole process that results in a moment. A season of consecration that results in an elevation and year of fulfilled promises. The moment is so big, overwhelming that I know it was God consecrating and blessing me for being able to focus and go through the process. God takes you through something sustained, called a season, only to do something immediately, such as elevate you and fulfill promises years in the making. That is the way God moves.

Here is a story I heard from a pastor about one of his members. A Christian man was presented with a proposal from his non-Christian father-in-law who was willing to put up money so the young man could go into business for himself. It sounded like a great opportunity, so with little hesitation he plunged right in. It wasn't long before the money coming in was substantially more than this man had ever made in the past, not to mention the heady experience of such quick "success". He was spending a lot less time at home with his wife and kids, and frequently missed church (though his family continued to attend) but he assured all concerned that he had everything under control. His absence from these important things was only temporary.

Once he had the business on its feet, things would get better. Soon though, he was working seven days a week. He had purchased several new vehicles to replace the old ones he had been using, and had made the down payment on an office space in a good location. He also hired a contractor to remodel portion of his home. It seemed that things were going better than they ever had, at least from a financial standpoint.

His frequent absences from the church meetings though, had now become constant. Several Christians who loved this man cautioned him of his neglect of his family and his spiritual life. "I'm doing fine" was always his answer. "As soon as I can get beyond this current raft of obligations, I'll return to the church." It didn't work out that way. In fact, in order to save money, he had his wife go to work in the business with him as a secretary and bookkeeper. They hired someone to watch the kids during the long hours they were away from home. Now no one was attending church and no one related was tending the home front.

The church leaders requests a meeting with the man and his wife but were politely told that there just wasn't enough time right now. So, months went by. Several Christians were so bold as to go visit this man at his office since that was the only place to catch him. "We're fine" was the response. "No need to worry about us. We'll get back to church someday." Soon though, there was no contact at all between this family and their Christian friends. The months turned into years. No one heard from them. Naturally, people moved on with their lives.

Then late one evening the wife called the minister of the church and told him that her husband was in jail. Could someone from the church please go down to the police station and help him? When the minister arrived he was surprised to find that the wife wasn't there. Apparently she had called from another location. There at the County Jail, through the two-way glass, the story came out.

The man started drinking when he found out that his wife was having an affair. After an angry confrontation he stormed out, climbed into his vehicle, and sped off into the night. At some point he ran down and killed a pedestrian along the road. Sitting there in the visitation room, the man poured out the rest of the story. The affair had been going on for over a year. He lost his head when he found out. Now he is charged with manslaughter.

Could the minister help him, he asked? Could God help him? He remembered something he had heard in a sermon one time about God's word having answers and the truth setting one free. Surely he needed some of that now! Could God get him out of this jam and give him his wife and family back?

If you were the minister, what would you tell this man? What could you offer to help? Is there some Bible verse somewhere that would take away all these problems? What answers could you offer? Sadly, there is a terrible truth looming here with awful implications. Do you know what it is? "Whatever a man sows, this he will also reap."

When God tells us that we will reap what we sow, he is not punishing us; he's telling us how things really are. Sometimes we DON'T reap what we sow because someone steps in and reaps the consequences for us. Children wait until the last minute to do their projects; the parents step in and make the choice to take over. What are the children learning? People who keep calling loved ones to bail them out of jail: what are they really learning?

Just as we can interfere with the law of gravity by catching a glass tumbling off the table, people can interfere with the Law of Cause and Effect by stepping in and rescuing irresponsible people. Rescuing a person from the natural consequences of his or her behavior enables them to continue in irresponsible behavior. We live in a society where people seem to no longer take responsibility for their choices in life. Life is about a series of choices, and we reap what we sow or do not sow.

What had this man sown? Neglect of his wife and family. Neglect of his spiritual life. Love of money that was out of balance with his love for God. He had gone from "seek first God's kingdom" to "don't seek His kingdom at all." What was he reaping? He got an extended jail sentence. His wife divorced him to go with her lover. His teenage children rebelled. He filed bankruptcy and lost his business. Eventually, because he couldn't make the payments, he lost his half of the house they had lived in. Again, if you were that minister, what would you tell this man?

The Bible does have answers to all of our problems. God has provided for us "all things pertaining to life and godliness" through the true knowledge of Christ (2 Peter 1:3). But please hear me on this: The answers God gives are mostly preventative rather than remedial. In other words, He tells us how to avoid these kinds of problems, not how to make them vanish when we have ignored His warnings.

Could this man repent of all his neglect, turn back to God, and restore his hope of eternal life? Yes, if the turning is genuine. Would such a move restore his wife and family and business? That is far less likely. Why? Here comes that awful law again: We reap what we sow! When we sow to the flesh we reap corruption. We reap things that shrivel, wither, spoil, and rot. Should this man be angry when God doesn't step in and take away all of his problems? Could he blame God for these troubles? Yes, he could, and many angrily blame Him in such cases. But the truth is this man can rightly blame only himself. God has published a book full of warnings about things like this. But that book is meaningless to people who don't pay attention and Focus on it. The book is the Word of God or the Bible. Is all lost then? Not necessarily. This man may still find hope in his life.

Establishing boundaries helps people stop interrupting the Law of sowing and reaping. Boundaries force the person who is doing the sowing to also do the reaping. Just confronting someone doesn't help. Telling them what we think about their behavior and that they need to change is really just NAGGING. They don't feel the need to change because their behavior is not causing them any pain. Confronting an irresponsible person is not painful to them; the truth of the matter is only consequences are.

If a person is wise, confronting them may change their behavior. But people caught in destructive patterns are usually not wise. They need to suffer consequences before they change their behavior. The Bible tells us it is worthless to confront foolish people: "Do not rebuke a mocker or he will hate you; rebuke a wise man and he will love you." (Prov. 9:8)

What does God do when we make bad choices? He gives us His love and presence and comfort as we live out the consequences. He doesn't condemn us and say, "You're such an idiot. You're so stupid! I told you that would happen. Now look at the mess you've made." He says instead, "I love you and I'll walk through this with you."

The truth is also that we reap more than we sow. This point is in the second part of the law of sowing and reaping. If we sow to the spirit (during this life) we will reap eternal life. Think of the proportionality between cause an effect there. What is it that you and I can do here and now to earn or equal the benefit of eternal life? Yet if we live for God here and now, in this relatively short span we call earthly life, we will receive much more than we ever put in. Live a relatively short time for God and you'll receive eternity with HIm.

Think about seeds. A single seed can grow a plant that produces hundreds or even thousands of seeds. A single bag of seeds can sow a whole field and produce hundreds of bags of new seed. We reap more than we sow. This is true in the positive sense, but it is also true in the negative. In the negative sense, there is a warning in the Old Testament book of Hosea, in 8:7, that says: "For they sow the wind, and they reap the whirlwind." The idea is that if we sow a little bit of evil we will reap a lot of evil. We sow a stiff breeze and we reap a tornado.

Think of the story I just told you. Had the man known the terrible things that would ultimately happen as a result of his choices, perhaps he would have thought about them more seriously in the beginning. No, it isn't wrong to go into business for yourself. Neither is it wrong to work long and hard - provided you don't neglect the things that are critically important, like your wife and your children and your God.

A single seed is such a tiny thing - so seemingly insignificant. A handful of tiny seeds is still not much. What harm could there possibly be in sowing them? They look so helpless lying there. Yes, that's how they look, but when you consider a seed, don't think of just one seed. Think of a harvest. Think of reaping a field because that's the way the law of sowing and reaping works.

Since I mentioned it in the earlier story, let's consider church attendance among the several issues involved. What difference does it make whether I come here and meet with the Saints, worship, and hear teaching from God's word? That stuff can seem so irrelevant to what I'm doing sometimes. Yeah, I know the pastors and preachers here at Imani say it's important, but many believe that we're all just too impressed with our own importance. Besides, as men and women of God what do we know, we probably never had a real job anyway. So we make decisions based on thinking that as a bishop I just want a crowd. So, if that is all it's about to you no wonder it's not that important.

Well, 1 Timothy 3:15 says, the church is the "pillar and support of the truth." What happens when you remove the support from something? Yes, you got it, it falls down! So is the church important? God created church as a place on earth accessible and congenial for being present to us, listening to us, and speaking to us on our home turf. It is also His gift to us, a place in our neighborhood for being present to God, listening to God and speaking to him. Church then is the place for ordinary people, like you and I, to gather locally, and have immediate, intimate, personal time with God, as He welcomes us into the company of Jesus, who is God with us, who embraces the human condition and speaks our language as He makes available time to be with us and sow necessary seed.

But I hear you out there saying, but it's just a seed! Surely it's not as significant as my career and my financial portfolio and house I need to remodel! If we had the time I could set aside the issue of church attendance and make the same point with the other important disciplines of the Christian life. They may seem insignificant and unimportant, but they're seeds - tiny seeds that become a harvest - tiny seeds that, if neglected, become an empty field where a harvest should have been when you needed it.

Focus now on what Paul says here in the text, "do not be deceived." We reap what we sow. We reap more than we sow. We reap only if we sow. As with the points I've already made, this has both a positive and negative application. We reap only if we sow can mean that if we don't put seeds sown to the Spirit into the ground we will get to the end of life and find we don't have eternal life. We may find even before the end of life that we don't have the strength we need to live effectively.

But again, I want to focus on the negative here. This statement holds an assurance that can provide security against ruining our lives. We reap only if we sow. If we don't sow the seeds of a bad habit, we'll never have to deal with the difficulties that result. If I don't allow myself to murmur, complain, and brood about difficult times, I'm far less likely to get caught in a downward spiral of depression. If I don't take that first drink, I won't ever - ever - become an alcoholic. If I don't flirt with members of the opposite sex, I won't be unfaithful to my spouse. If I don't plant the seed, I won't have to deal with a rotten harvest. If the choices I make and the chances I take have spiritual boundaries and carefully selected seeds sown in responsible ways then my harvest will be plentiful and my promises fulfilled. Only the foolish, move God's boundaries for their lives.

I think this is what was behind Jesus' instructions in Matthew 5:27-28 when he said, "You have heard that it was said, 'You shall not commit adultery'; but I say to you, that everyone who looks on a woman to lust for her has committed adultery with her already in his heart."

What Jesus was doing here was moving the battle line against unfaithfulness back into the heart where the seed of it begins. Thoughts germinate and grow in the heart long before they become actions. If we strive to control the thoughts, if we attack and master the problem on that level which, though difficult, is not as difficult as dealing with physical act, we minimize the potential for wrong actions. Life is far less difficult and complicated. That's what I meant earlier when I said that the answers God gives us in His word are more preventative than remedial. It's much easier to deal with impure thoughts than it is to deal with the impact of a betrayal on a marriage and the results of a broken covenant.

Jesus was speaking from the masculine perspective in Matthew 5, but this principle of gaining control of the thoughts applies to all of us, male or female. It's a lot easier to crush a snake's egg than it is to contend with a four-foot viper! A tiny spark can be extinguished with a pinch. Putting out a destructive forest fire takes millions of dollars and risks many lives. We reap what we sow. We reap more than we sow. We reap only if we sow.

We get deceived when we think that since we've sown some seeds and seemingly gotten away with it, we are somehow immune or exempt. As the familiar modern proverb says, "Some folks sow bad seeds all week, then come to church and pray for a crop failure." It doesn't work that way unfortunately.

It takes time to get a harvest. In the positive sense, we must patiently sow those spiritual seeds and be confident that it will all be worth it. If we do we will see some of the results in the here-and-now and some beyond this life. The same point (some will show up here and now and some in the afterlife) is also true. Paul made that point in 1 Tim 5:24 where he said, "The sins of some men are quite evident, going before them to judgment; for others, their sins follow after." Some reaping as a result of sowing to the flesh will come in this life, some in the next.

The idea that the sowing usually comes some time after the reaping also shows up in Ecclesiastes 8:11, which says, "Because the sentence against an evil deed is not executed quickly, therefore the hearts of the sons of men among them are given fully to do evil." Because there is a delay between cause and effect, we get the mistaken idea that there is no effect. Yet my point is that we reap later than we sow.

In the story I shared with you earlier, the choices the husband made at the start of his new business didn't seem to be that harmful. On the contrary, they actually seemed to benefit him. In fact, such a one could easily conclude, early on that "God must approve because He seems to be blessing my business." Only after some years did the true harvest of neglect come due. And it was a bitter harvest.

We reap what we sow. We reap more than we sow. We reap only if we sow. We reap later than we sow. We reap until we have harvested what we sow. Looking back at Galatians 6:9: "And let us not lose heart in doing good, for in due time we shall reap if we do not grow weary."

Paul was definitely speaking from the positive angle when he spoke of reaping the results of "doing good." And it's a good lesson. For those of us who are focusing on sowing to the Spirit, while people around us seemingly get away with sowing to the flesh, the road can get long. It would be very easy to say, "I think I'll let go. I'm getting tired. Let somebody else do this for awhile." Paul reminds those who are thinking this way not to quit. The effort will be worth it "in due time."

But there is another possible application for his words. I asked you earlier what you would say if you were the minister talking to that man in jail who was losing all he had worked so hard to accomplish. Here is how I might deal with his questions.

First, I would have to tell him the truth about the law of sowing and reaping. You mean you would tell him that he was to blame for his own problems? That would be cruel! How could you possibly hit him so hard when he is down? Be assured that I would do this as kindly as possible, but if I don't tell him the truth then he will end up blaming others for the problems that only he can resolve. You don't help someone by blaming other people for one's own wrongdoing.

Secondly, I would tell him to return to God with his whole heart. No half-hearted turnaround would do. He got into these problems by pushing God to the bottom of his priority list until his Creator was completely off his list. He must admit his sin and throw himself upon God's mercy. If he were truly a believer and disciple of Christ in the first place, this repentance and return would remove the eternal penalty for his wrong. If he returns to God with his whole heart, he can still be saved. Though this man seems awash in his earthly problems, eternity is really the greater jeopardy.

Thirdly, I would lovingly tell him the truth about what was ahead. He would have to reap the earthly consequences of his sowing. God would not likely remove that. It would probably be a long haul. He would have to serve his jail sentence. His wife might never come back. His children might never forgive him. But his one greatest chance of any of these things happening would be a full return to His God including a complete rearrangement of his priorities.

Fourthly, I would tell him what Paul says here in our text: "And let us not lose heart in doing good, for in due time we shall reap if we do not grow weary." Though the bitter reaping might be long and difficult, if he continues to deal with it responsibly, while not putting more seeds of the flesh into the ground, eventually the reaping would be over. All of the nasty harvesting would be gone. This could come in this life. If not, it would surely come in the next. But during this time of bitter reaping he must resist the temptation to get angry and sow other evil things in his frustration, which he would later have to reap.

Finally, I would tell him these things once. Then I would tell them to him again and again, as long as he would listen, because you can be sure that Satan would be whispering in his other ear the very opposite. "It's just too much." "It's hopeless." "All is lost." "You're doomed." Give up! It's over! "God can't help you." The name of the game, folks, is deception, and at such times it comes on hard, long, and fast, brought to you by the enemy of our souls.

Here is where the devil comes in strong, loud and wrong, not necessarily in the original decision, but in the response to hope in Christ. He comes in to ask the discouraging question: "Do you really think God loves you enough, to help you now that you've made the wrong decision?"

For the man I described it would be a long haul - a long journey, probably with much heartache. But it would not be a life without hope because Paul says in our text, "in due time we shall reap if we do not grow weary." In due time, the reaping would be over.

Ancient Israel began reaping what she had sown at the onset of the Babylonian Captivity. For 70 years she languished in obscurity and defeat. But ultimately, when the reaping was over, God restored her. When the children of Israel came out of Egypt the first place God led them was to Marah the Oasis of bitterness before he could lead them to Elim the place of 12 wells and 70 palm trees. He can do that for us, too. "In due time, we shall reap if we do not grow weary." This is the season of consecrating our flesh. While we may reap painful consequences of past choices, we will reap the harvest of fulfilled promises in the next.

The choices you make; the chances you take!

FOCUS

"Who Do People Say That I Am?"

As we prepare for the first meeting of our fledging organization, The Bridge Network Covenant Fellowship of Associated Churches and Independent Ministries, the first thing that strikes me as important is the question: What should we call the meeting? In my years of attending meetings, I am always amazed with their names. You will recognize these terms from your own experience: conferences, seminars, meetings, etc.

Rarely do we get invitations to a "Summit." Why is that? According to the definition, it is usually for the heads of something as in states or countries. Of course, we have heard heads of corporations refer to meetings as summits as well. So part of the definition would depend on whose there.

A second part of the definition implies people who attend summits are decision makers of the highest order. Things get done at a summit; the attendees don't need to call people home or call the office to get permission to act. Finally, summits signal the importance of the issues at hand. If you have a summit on something, it must be important.

Summits can be powerful events, but bringing all the right people together, in the right place and in the right way, sure isn't easy. We are convening the influential leaders and stakeholders of our churches and independent ministries to declare purpose and bold aspirations. We invite provocative ideas; facilitate dialogue; encourage breakthrough thinking; celebrate shared vision for new opportunities; to work, worship and watch change happen as we build bridges into changing times.

I recognize the need to reintroduce myself to many of you, now that I am a Bishop in the Lord's church, consecrated and elevated by Bishops representing the National Joint College of Bishops. I am committed to being in covenant with God and those of you who would open your hearts to join me in this new work for the kingdom of God.

Likewise we began a new venture, The Shelter White Institute of Biblical Study. Our first class produced 36 graduates with certificates in Biblical Study. The prestigious Doctor of Divinity Degree was awarded to me by the Board of our Institute partner Promise Christian University and Seminary.

With all that has been going on I find I have a need to refocus: To reintroduce myself as we go into changing dimensions of God's glory, as we prepare to Sit at the Table of God's Favor, and Enjoy His Fulfilled Promises. Jesus asked his disciples the question: 'Who do people say that I am?" Some said you are Jeremiah, one of the prophets, some say Elijah, etc. But then the question was raised, "But who do you say that I am?

I am as challenged, dear community, by the awesomeness of the responsibility of reintroduction just as the Black church is challenged by the need to represent herself as relevant in these difficult and changing times. People are trying to understand what being in covenant is as Christians and married couples. Who do people say the church is, especially the Black church? The mainstream information systems appear to be preoccupied with black failure, black death, and black pathology. When the truth of the matter is we have a lot of black life, black creativity, black critical intelligence and consecrated imagination that goes unreported and unappreciated even by those of us who should greatly value these gifts. The challenge is they are not very visible.

Our generation appears to be caught up in the flow of violence, divorce, discouragement and depression and we need to understand the issues of our times and the covenant it seems to have made with our demise; from the struggles over land, ideology, identity, the concept of marriage, economics, the theology of compromise that are affecting the lives and promises of the people we serve. But will we likewise celebrate our victories not just our victimization and change our FOCUS? This is what I believe Jesus was doing when He asked, 'Who do you say that I am?"

There is a dynamic of our times, communities and consciousness where a group of people have come to life, after 500 years of not being heard from. We are still working to reach some balance, within our society, to this recent phenomenon. What do we do when we are lifted out of our dead and unconscious existence and brought into the light of promise, purpose, power and possibilities? Do we celebrate or castigate? Establish a covenant or compromise? Who do we say that we are?

When you hear voices smothered for so long what kind of sound do you encounter? So the question is "are we willing to be patient with our own voices, visions, and victories" as we work through the seasons of our consecrations and awakenings to be in covenant with our promises? Or will unreasonable expectations take us to places of impatience, impotence or self-importance shaping our work, will and worship?

What relevant message should we preach and present to those experiencing our times and moving into the promises of a fulfilled future as primarily black people, communities, families and churches? What should our focus be? What will lift us and not drop us further into the pit of despair, distraction, dysfunction, disconnection or discouragement?

Our people have had a legacy of being in covenant with independence. This independence was prescribed primarily by situations we as a black people, believers and nonbelievers alike, had forced upon us. The so-called black church as we now are experiencing it, along with our community's concept of marriage has existed through the struggles of historic segregation and discrimination. We have been in an historic covenant of circumstances with her since we arrived as a people on the shores of America. When one does not have shoes and no one is willing to give you any, one will by necessity have to adapt and invent some. Necessity is the mother of invention.

The challenge of today's black church is to covenant with the people they are to serve; and its most pressing need is to move to presenting a vision and passion for a sincere alternative life we call a life in Christ. That life transcends, overcomes or utterly destroys the life of dysfunction, devastation, distraction, disconnection and destruction presently being offered to us as people of God and a community of faith who are historically Black. It is a pressing matter of being called out; in the world but not of the world. We are to be against the world, not compromised by the world; or even the traditions given to us through our historic struggles as we adapted to make shoes to walk out our faith in covenant. We must not be well adjusted to injustice but maladjusted to injustice. We are to be the salt poured out of the salt shaker into a world of injustice, insensitivity and lack of intimacy; to preserve the love, joy, peace, and power to believe not only in the God who is handling the shaker, but in ourselves while being purposefully poured out. People should know us by our authentic fruit and not the distorted opinions of simple and insincere minds, leveled to the place of distorted values, visions and victories.

It is important to understand the legitimacy of the Bishopric from which I reintroduce myself and the Adjutancy and the set helps that support the office of the Bishop to the church universal and its place in the legacy and legitimacy of its covenant with the Black church. Unfortunately, there are those who have defiled the titles of each office within the church universal and specifically the Black church.

Well! Who do people say that I am? Here is something sent to me by one of our members and I believe this identifies those in covenant with God and His church.

I AM

- A Child of God (Romans 8:16)
- Redeemed from the Hand of the Enemy (Psalms 107:2)
- Forgiven (Colossians 1:13,14)
- Saved by Grace through Faith (Ephesians 2:8)
- Justified (Romans 5:1)
- Sanctified (II Corinthians 5:17)
- A New Creature (II Corinthians 5:17)
- Partaker of His Divine Nature (II Peter 1:4)
- Redeemed from the Curse of the law (Galatians 3:13)

- Delivered from the Powers of Darkness (Colossians 1:13)
- Led by the Spirit of God (Romans 8:14)
- A Son of God (Romans 8:14)
- Kept in safety wherever I go (Psalms 91:11)
- Getting All My Needs Met by Jesus (Philippians 4:19)
- Casting All My Cares on Jesus (I Peter 5:7)
- Strong in the Lord and in the Power of His Might (Ephesians 6:19)
- Doing All Things Through Christ Who Strengthens Me (Philippians 4:13)
- An Heir of God and a Joint Heir with Jesus (Romans 8:17)
- Heir to the Blessings of Abraham (Galatians 3:13,14)
- Observing and Doing the Lord's Commandments (Deuteronomy 28:12)
- Blessed Coming in and Blessed Going out (Deuteronomy 28:6)
- An Heir of Eternal Life (I John 5:11,12)
- Blessed with All Spiritual Blessings (Ephesians 1:3)
- Healed by His Stripes (I Peter 2:24)
- Exercising My Authority over the Enemy (Luke 10:19)
- Above only and Not Beneath (Deuteronomy 28:13)
- More than a Conqueror (Romans 8:37)
- Establishing God's Word Here on Earth (Matthew 16:19)

- An Overcomer by the Blood of the Lamb and the Word of My Testimony (Revelations 12:11)
- Daily Overcoming the Devil (I John 4:4)
- Not Moved by What I see (II Corinthians 4:18)
- Walking by Faith and Not by Sight (II Corinthians 5:7)
- Casting Down Vain Imaginations (II Corinthians 10:4,5)
- Bringing Every Thought into Captivity (II Corinthians 10:5)
- Being Transformed by Renewing My Mind (Romans 12:1,2)
- A Laborer Together with God (I Corinthians 3:9)
- The Righteousness of God in Christ (II Corinthians 5:21)
- An Imitator of Jesus (Ephesians 5:1)
- The Light of the World (Matthew 5:14)
- Blessing the Lord at All Times and continually Praising the Lord with My Mouth (Psalms 34:1)

I am also humbly in covenant with a number of you who have purposed to support me as your Bishop and Bridge Network partner. Well, what is a Covenant anyway? When was the last time you heard people in the church talk about this thing called covenant? Are our marriages covenants or have they now become like the world, a reality television program? The covenants of God are the cornerstone of the Bible and yet very few in our churches are familiar with its meaning or its application in our relationship with God and who people say that we the people of God are.

I believe one of the reasons our culture avoids words such as "summit," and "covenant" is because it is a commitment. Our society today in general does not like commitments. Years ago, it was not uncommon for one to be born, marry, and die in one community, attending one school, one church and hold one job within that community. Because of this there was a great sense of commitment. This commitment could be seen in how the family cared for its members, children, parents, grandparents, etc. Also, an employer cared for his employees and the employees took care of the employer in return. We respected our government and our country and many among us fought with our lives to protect them.

We can see from the current events that this is no longer the case. Today, we have just as many divorces as we have marriages even more so it seems in the black church. Older family members, no longer able to care for themselves are in homes for the elderly so they are not a burden on the rest of the family. When did we start throwing away babies and putting our elderly into uncaring institutions, because we are too busy to take care of them as a fulfillment of our covenant as family?

In today's big business, employees are only numbers to the employer; and employees leave the employer the moment a better offer comes along. The respect for our government has fallen, to the point where the flag is burned and the presidency is devalued because a Black man occupies the Oval office. The crime rate in our country shows the disrespect we have for one another and authority. The only commitment that we commit to today is to our own desires and happiness. We will do what is necessary and go wherever is needed to make ourselves happy. We will even break the eternal commitment of marriage just because we want to experience happiness with someone new. The most tragic loss is that we, as a people have forgotten the God of the Bible, the God who created us and gave us life; the God who made an eternal covenant with us. We are no longer a people who serve God and our fellow man; instead we serve ourselves and our image management. I feel there is reason enough for a summit of church leaders to chart a new course for a fulfilled promise, how about you?

Many in our Churches, worship God, pray to him and read from his word, but have excluded him from the rest of their life. We do not have the commitment to God that HE wants from us. God gave his people his eternal word, the Bible, which contains the Word of Truth and Life that God, has asked his people to obey. Within the Bible are special holy days to remind us of who He is and who we are in Him. The problem is that these Holy orders and ordinances are found in the First Covenant which Christians call, the "Old Testament' and dismiss as only for the Jews and not for us in the 'New Testament' time.

Our Bible has two parts, the First and New Covenant or what we call "The Old and New Testaments. The First Covenant is the story about God's covenant with man and the New Covenant is the continuing story and renewal of the covenant relationship between God and man. They were given to us so we might know who we are.

Ask the average Christian to define the differences between the First and New Covenants and he will probably say: "The 'Old Testament' is the 'law' God gave to the Jews. They were required to observe the Saturday Sabbath, observe holidays like the Passover feast and the Day of Atonement, perform sacrifices, abstain from certain foods, etc. When 'Jesus' died on the cross he did away with the 'law'. The 'New Testament' on the other hand is for Christians and teaches we are under Grace and it does not require us to keep the 'law' of the 'Old Testament'. Although the 'Old Testament' has good stories with certain truths for us today, it is the 'New Testament' that we live by".

But you see their understanding of the First and New Covenants differs from what the Bible actually teaches. There is a saying that says; "The New Testament (Covenant) is in the Old Testament (first Covenant) concealed; and the Old Testament (first Covenant) is in the New Testament (Covenant) revealed". The entire Gospel message can be taught from the First Covenant, the Old Testament scriptures. In fact, this is what the writers of the New Covenant did. They only had the First Covenant or Old Testament to teach the Gospel since the New Covenant or Testament had not yet been written. As I mentioned, the First Covenant is quoted in the New Covenant, a total of 343 times. Every teaching in the New Covenant is in the First Covenant. Paul believed the First Covenant scriptures to be very important as he said; "I believe everything that agrees with the Law (Old Testament or First Covenant) and that which is written in the Prophets" (Acts 24:14).

Do the New Covenant scriptures supersede the First Covenant scriptures? Or do they agree with each other, especially when it comes to the Law in First Covenant? The truth is that the New Covenant teaches more about the Law than we ever thought. If the teachings of the First Covenant and the Law are valid today, why aren't our churches teaching it? Who do people say that we are?

When we look at the names and titles of God's People, Israel, they were:

- A People set apart
- A Holy People
- A Community set apart
- A Holy Assembly
- The Descendants of Abraham
- Israel
- The Chosen People
- A Holy Nation
- The people of God
- Children of God
- Sheep
- Brothers

Each of these names and titles is in the New Testament (Covenant) and is attributed to the believers. Not to a new church of Gentile believers, but to Israel and the Gentiles who enter into the covenant with them.

The first two covenants of the Bible are the marriage covenant and the flood covenant or promise. Although these covenants are not directly related to God's redemptive plan for mankind, the marriage covenant gives us an example of how a covenant is intended to work. It also gives us an opportunity to see how Satan has desecrated it. Although the Genesis account of the creation of the man and woman does not call this union a covenant, the prophet Malachi understood it as such when he wrote "the wife of your marriage covenant" (2:14).

The covenant of marriage is between a man and a woman, as it says in Genesis 2:20-22, "But for Adam no suitable helper was found. So the LORD God caused the man to fall into a deep sleep; and while Adam was sleeping, God took one of Adam's ribs and closed up the place with flesh. Then the LORD God made a woman from the rib he had taken out of the man, and he brought her to the man".

In the wedding vows, each member of the party gives their promises to the other. These promises usually include; love, care and obedience. Marriage is to be an unconditional covenant. This means that there are to be no conditions placed on the covenant. Jesus said in Matthew 19:6; "Therefore, what God has joined together, let man not separate".

A marriage is binding on each party as long as the two live, as is said in our wedding ceremonies today; "Till death us do part". Paul said in 1 Corinthians 7:39; "A woman is bound to her husband as long as she lives". Did anybody explain this to Kim and her husband?

Each culture is a little different, but for us we use a ring as the sign of the covenant. The ring is a daily reminder of the promises made in the covenant. As I reintroduce myself as a Bishop in the Lord's church I do so wearing a ring that signifies my covenant as a daily reminder that I am married to God and Kathy. Who do people say that I am? Who do people say the church is? Who do people say you are?

When talking about our Bridge Network covenant we quote Fannie Lou Hamer who said during the civil rights era, "there are two things we ought never forget. Never forget where you come from and always give praises to the bridges that carried you over."

See you on the bridge!

FOCUS

A Season of Consecration as Chosen Vessels

In my role as the founding pastor of a growing church, and Presiding Bishop of a fledgling network of associated churches and independent ministries every day I see the hurt the people of God are experiencing. Especially in the lives of the chosen vessels called women. There is a reason why some people cannot lead some of today's churches. It is because most people cannot identify with things like pain, disappointment and bitterness that come with ministry that is not in the sphere of their understanding and sensitivity. When someone tries to help them understand that everybody was not raised like them, and doesn't see life the way they see it they resist, resent and run back to traditional perspectives to hide. The truth is everybody has perspective. We have a perspective on life based on where we were raised, how we were raised, who raised us, and our experiences all work to cast perspective. It is how we view life. But do we really pursue God's perspective without attempting to mix it up with church culture? The same is true for how we see ministry as leaders, their pain in serving and the question of "Are women truly chosen vessels of God?" Or are they just helpers of men?

There is a painful church culture. People raised in very traditional churches often see God in very strict traditional ways. One of them is women can't be leaders in churches as chosen vessels. This was recently shown to me while in Iowa when I was immediately confronted with this question upon sitting down for dinner "what do I think about women preachers I was asked? This was coming from a former first lady. People raised in some of our new movement churches see God as a crazy but caring God; meaning they have a perspective of God that traditional churches and people often can't understand and won't relate to. Your environment determines your perspective.

Because of this, we see different cultures expressed in very different ways, often giving us competing perspectives mostly along cultural lines and too often dividing men and women. When you have a level of influence, you have no idea the amount of pressure placed on you to go in one way or another in certain things like politics, how we raise our children and even how we express worship to God. The most damaging in my opinion is how we receive women in ministry and sadly even in the challenges of relationships. When you become a representative of the kingdom you begin to develop the perspective that understands that it is bigger than any earthly alignment, culture or political affiliation or relational perspective one can have. We must establish kingdom connections as the yeast and the dough that saturates everything.

What does the word of God say about the purpose and the place of women? Well, I discovered upon investigation that she is truly a chosen vessel of God. The problem is whether or not she is seeking holiness or happiness. Holiness cost her perspective. Happiness may cost her His presence. While women in churches everywhere are trying to make everybody happy: their husbands, pastors, church leaders, families, and other woman are they losing perspective of what they are truly chosen to be and become in Christ? Are they bearing the Image of God or just seeking to identify traditionally with a cultural perspective that excludes them, expects them to be what they want them to be, and then dismisses them and their pain, bitterness and hopes? Looking into the future as perspective for focus next year –we discover we are entering into the year of fulfilled promises! As chosen vessels in pursuit of His holiness, "Woman of God are you positioning yourselves to fulfill the Godly purpose for your life?

Psalm 27:13-14, and paraphrasing it a little will help us to better relate to its implication. The Psalmist is saying, "I would have lost heart or "I had fainted," "unless I had believed" or "I'd like to give up on life." The psalmist as a chosen vessel of God's holiness had reached a breaking point, but he would discover that God could still hold him together.

The psalmist wakes up that morning sluggish and tired like far too many of us in our churches. He hasn't slept much, because what he is going through has him so uptight that he has developed a bad case of what I like to call "spiritual insomnia." He is scheduled to be the worship leader in his church today, but he wonders how he can possibly hold himself together in front of all the people. He has reached a "breaking point" and feels that he could crack at any moment. He knows he is just a few steps away from losing his mind. His life is a mess; he is burned out, and doesn't believe he has the strength to hold out one more day. After debating with himself for a while, he decides he had better go on to church. With his last ounce of strength, he goes to church and takes his place as worship leader. He takes his position and begins the hymn of affirmation" verses 1-6, "The Lord is my light and my salvation, whom shall I fear? . . . therefore I will offer in his tabernacle sacrifices of joy; I will sing, yes, I will sing praises unto the Lord."

When it is time to offer the sacrifice of joy, he realizes he has no joy to offer. When it is time to sing praises, he discovers he has no praise to give. So, rather than continue going through the motions pretending to have joy and praise, he is moved in his spirit to pour out the pain in his life and open his wound before God. He cries out to God for help (V. 7-13). What the psalmist does in church that day transforms his breaking point into a turn around! The psalmist exposes his pain, expresses his problem, then encounters God's promise. This is what chosen vessels in pursuit of His holiness must do.

When we look at the picture God presents as he identifies his chosen vessels you find that intensity grows from the very beginning of the text. By the time we leave the text of beginnings in Genesis we come into more and more issues relating to women and their pain, problems and our lack of perspective concerning their use as chosen vessels of God in the earth. Whether it is barrenness, hostility, bitterness, attitudes and whether or not to be used by God, we see the intensity mounting with each woman presented. From Eve, to Sarah, to Hagar, to Leah, to Tamar, to Jochebed, to Miriam, to Zipporah, to Rahab; sadly as woman, none of them made it to the Promised Land. But the question is were they chosen vessels used by God in pursuit of His Holiness?

There is a strained church culture. We are living in an age and church experience where we do not expect much from our worship experience mainly because we do not expect much from our worship leaders who mostly are men. Therefore, we don't get much from it or at least not the complete picture of promise. Especially when we continue to separate what God has brought together as His chosen vessels of Holiness as His image bearers.

We do not express or encourage others to expose their problems or pain in worship, and some of us act like we do not have any problems, which in fact, is a false presentation being offered weekly in churches everywhere. Women are painfully ignored by men who don't have the perspective that they are just as capable and needed to fulfill God's promise and purpose. The bible says, 'confess your faults one to another and pray for one another." Our pain as leaders, both men and women, can be a point of worship and our problem can put us in a powerful position for ministry. Instead, we hide until we can't take it any longer then bleed all over the people till they can't take it anymore and everybody just gives up. How sad.

We are trained and taught as ministry and worship leaders, both men and women, to hide our hurt and to cover our cries, so that people will think that we have it all together. Ministry couples fight like cats and dogs before church, and then sit together like they are always loving and caring towards one another. Ministry wives sit up in our churches feeling like widows with a husband that has no time, no tenderness, no intention of seeing her pain or hearing her cries, and no place for intimacy because of the strain of ministry. We pretend to be strong when we are really using our last ounce of strength just to get up and come to church. This week, chosen vessel, as you prepare to pursue His holiness why not expose your pain and experience God's healing and like this psalmist find the key to victory which is to position yourself to "Wait on the Lord!"

Galatians 4:1 says, "Think of it this way. If a father dies and leaves an inheritance for his young children, those children are not much better off than slaves until they grow up, even though they actually own everything their father had."

We are truly God's very own children. Chosen vessels who should be in pursuit of His holiness. Paul is saying here that their condition is that they own an inheritance but have not come to maturity yet. Maturity is not in calendar years but growing up in the things of God. Even the elderly are not as mature as they think just because they have reached an older age but are yet immature in the way they conduct their lives. The bible says that growing up means to make good decisions in the things of God. Things like not living in the past and letting it dictate your future. As chosen vessels we must become people who can forgive even though people have mistreated you. Don't make decisions out of emotions; become people who are slow to speak and quick to hear.

Sadly, what we find all too often is far too many people are lacking in these things in the church; making it hard to get along. People can't agree on anything. An attitude of self-righteousness reigns supreme and people seem to find it hard to be saved. Maybe the issue is they truly haven't been set apart yet or mature in the things of God. This goes for both men and women.

Here is the truth, we need to grow up! The church needs to grow up and mature so we may enjoy the grace, extend the glory, and establish the throne of the kingdom of God and come into our year of fulfilled promises. Galatians 4:2 says they have to obey their guardians until they reach whatever age their father set. God has a prearranged place for you and me to grow up in. Paul says "I labor till Christ be formed in you". This prearranged place is one of consecration we call justification by faith as opposed to works. It is a heart conditioned place. Not a works applied place.

As I try to recover from being laid up with a collapsed lung and persistent bronchitis, that feels like I blew out a tire; God seems to be telling me that we have made a spiritual shift from doctrinal concerns, and traditional perspective to personal exhortation that we might fulfill our promised inheritance through a season of realizing we are justified only by the grace of God and ought to enjoy it.

Briefly, just to call to your mind the conversation the Apostle Paul is having as he shifts from theologian to a pastor whose heart cries out to his people, both men and women under his care. Paul had established, on his very first missionary tour with his friend Barnabas, various churches in an area known as Galatia. In several cities there, Derbe, Lystra, Iconium, and Antioch, he had established churches. These captured my imagination as we begin the process of establishing formally our Bridge Network Covenant Fellowship of Associated Churches and independent ministries. Here is a draft of our new seal. The symbols are the bridge, the globe, the cross and the rainbow.

Paul establishes his network of churches on the basis of salvation by grace through faith alone as he reaches out to the world with his message of Good News; and as a guardian of the faith of the people he served, he also told them to be focused as chosen and consecrated vessels in pursuit of God's holiness. No sooner had he left there, some Jews from Jerusalem arrived and claimed to be Christians, then immediately told everyone that it wasn't enough just to believe to be saved, but you had to get circumcised and keep the law. Just like some Christians today would rather offer rules than the heart of relationships as evidence of their inheritance as God's children and church representing His body. Truthfully, beloved, we can have a collapsed heart condition and call it faithfully serving God as His chosen vessels.

Word got back to Paul that these people had been sold this particular lie, and so Paul wrote Galatians as a circular letter, to be passed among these churches, to inform them that these Judaizers (as he calls them), those who want to impose Judaistic ritual and ceremony, were wrong. They had the wrong but traditional perspective. He told them they needed to cling to the salvation offered through grace in Christ as chosen vessels of God's holiness and bearers of His image. That is the message of Galatians. This is our message of Focus in this season of consecration.

Now, up to this point in Galatians 4:12, Paul has been handling the situation academically. It is very impersonal. He has been handling it like a scholar with a tremendous intellect who is just marshaling his arguments. Or like a lawyer who comes into court and simply defends his case without any real concern for people he is defending. Or, perhaps, like a theologian who is just amassing all sorts of Scriptural knowledge to prove his theological point. You might say its all head and no heart. He doesn't even bother to say any kind of greeting to the people; he just fires away at them. It's very much academic and very absent of anything personal. Up until now there has been no heart but all head.

This season we've seen tremendous conviction, tremendous intellectual and spiritual powers in operation, tremendous knowledge of the Episcopal things bringing us into new knowledge and awareness of church order and structure all great but we must be mindful of all head and no heart. Paul here is battling to preserve a God-authored dogma, or doctrine. He has seemed very detached, he has preferred truth to friendship, fact to fellowship, and he has preferred principles to people up to this point. Warning! If you identify with this maybe you have a collapsed heart condition and need to Re-Focus your head struggle for a change of heart.

Forgive me beloved where I have been all head and no heart, all instruction with too much insensitivity to your challenges, obstacles and fears. Truly, I care so very much for your well-being and your salvation. I want you to know that I too must remain focused as well; as a bishop, even more so, to become a chosen vessel of His holiness and His image bearer.

For Paul everything changes in Galatians 4:12. It even begins with the word 'brethren'. This is the first leak in his academic tank, as it were. This is the first time that anything that even smacks of personal concern as opposed to academics or theology begins to seep out. This is what "The Theology of Focus" and these series of writings have been concerned with. How is our faith in God's will for us and our love for one another being realized and practiced in a real sense within the church?

Is our sense of obedience to this calling as a body of believers, chosen vessels of His holiness called together by God's grace real or imagined? Do we commit to one another and God's call on our lives and ministries serving both men and women to not only equip the saints for the work of the ministry, but by being concerned for their welfare as we live out our lives together in unity "till we all come together in the unity of the faith" and become true servants of God for His glory? This takes both head and heart to be realized in the lives of both men and women equally and our calling as chosen vessels in pursuit of His Holiness in this season of consecration in order to enter a year of fulfilled promises.

It seems as though he has just banged out theological arguments and his fury has run its course in defending his case. By this time, his anger is gone, his frustration is gone, to a point, and his rhetoric is all fired out. Now, he comes down and slips from the doctrinal to the personal. Likewise, like me he seems to have blown a tire, his lung collapses and now sitting on the side of the road realizes that without the heart of the matter being addressed, what has it all been for? With my lungs not working properly, my concern is while I was on fire did my heart touch anyone or just my rhetoric. Was I talking and no one listening; and now when I slowdown is my heart now heard louder as it beats though I can't speak as loud. What beloved has it all been for?

Brethren, beloved, do you hear me and feel my heart for you and this ministry? Do you know how much I care and do you know how much I need you to fulfill not only your promise but mine as well? In fact, the words from verse 12 through verse 20 are the strongest words of personal affection that Paul ever uses. There is even one term that he uses for the Galatians that he never uses for anyone else, the term that is included in verse 19. It begins, "My little children." He brings himself down to speaking like a loving mother, "Of whom I have birth pains again until Christ be formed in you." Now we begin to see that the man is not just arguing academics, but his heart condition is jointed completely in the image of God that can only be expressed fully by both genders coming together as he expresses he cares about them as people.

Seen through the perspective of a loving mother; he truly wants them to become chosen vessels in pursuit of His holiness.

You know, the term 'brethren' in verse 12, he kind of slides into it, but by the time we reach verse 19 and he uses the diminutive 'my little children', he is just pouring out personal love. Latin and Greek languages both use diminutives as terms of very deep affection, and that is what you see here.

I think it's true too that there must be this side to every man of God like myself, there must be, as well as the tremendous strength of conviction, a gentleness needed to create the heart history that nurtures and preserves the vessels with a perspective given through the image of woman as mothers, daughters, sisters, lovers and leaders. Paul had an experience when he arrived in Thessalonica, which he described in I Thessalonians 2:7. He says, "We were gentle among you as a nursing mother cherishes her children, being affectionately desirous of you." So aside from the strength, conviction, tremendous intellect, and the ability to put together an argument and defend it, there was the warmth and personal character that I pray we have seen in my attempt to lead this flock and establish the throne of God in this place we have come to call Imani.

Of course, this isn't just Paul, but Paul got this from Jesus, because Jesus was this way. It was the same Jesus who cleansed the temple, on His way to presenting Himself as a cathedra or place we look to as His throne who lifted up the children and said, "Suffer the little ones to come unto me, and forbid them not, for of such is the kingdom of Heaven." It is the same Jesus who is described in the book of Revelation as a lion and a lamb. In fact, the Apostle Paul even ascribed his own gentleness to the fact of the example of Christ. In II Corinthians 10:1, "I, Paul, myself beseech you by the meekness and gentleness of Christ." In other words, he had appropriated, as it were, the gentleness of Christ for himself. Maybe things collapse in our lives to get us to Focus our pursuits not only with conviction but with humility and gentleness of heart.

At the end of the book of Philippians, in 4:5, he says, "Let your gentleness be known unto all men." He calls upon all Christians to be strong in conviction, this is the manly perspective but also to be gentle, which is the woman's perspective. This is what is often missing in our churches with its traditional approach to leadership and ministry. So, as we look at these verses, I can relate to this from my standpoint, I'll illustrate it as a pastor. There are times when you're preaching, and I'm sure this happens to everyone; you're firing away and building your rhetoric and logic, and driving to a point. Then, all of a sudden, you've made your point and come off sermonizing, and you say, "Now look, people. I'm talking to you and here's how it is. I care about you." This is taking the message to a place of ministry. That's Paul. He isn't sermonizing in verses 12-20, he's not really even writing, he's just pouring out his heart like I am attempting to do here for you.

When that place has been REACHED God releases things that he can bless you and I with, what He does then is put you under – not over - guardians - call them stewards of God's grace until the time appointed by Father God. He has assigned relationships to grow you up. This is the focus for our season of consecration.

Real mentorship is not impressed with you, because you have nothing they need. Here is the truth of the matter; one must never submit oneself to those who need what you have because you can be used that way. People who have been hurt in church usually have been hurt because they feel they've been used.

But when God orders a relationship it is with someone who operates on a greater level than you to be your mentor. My mentors don't need what I have. Neither do you. This allows us to not drain one another dry but we can share the well of blessing drawing on one another with both head and heart as chosen vessels and bearers of His image.

God will sometimes make you be around people that will make you grow up. They may get on your nerves but they are a blessing. The people that like everything you do may not be the ones that care like you think they do. The next generation does not get God with your song! To them all TV's are flat. They've never experience anything else. All TV's then to them become irrelevant as they move on to newer and newer technology. The church all head and no heart wants them to care about that which they have no guidance or experience in and will not ever see in their lifetime like a rotary phone or rabbit ears on a television. You can never reach their heart with these things.

There are ways to say you don't connect to another generation without saying it. We must focus and re-educate ourselves by being around different groups. Things change and relevance is an important aspect of vision. What you can't see or won't see doesn't make it irrelevant it's just out of focus many times.

Re-education to become aware of a new generations sound and sensitivities is a must. This generation can by the nature of their mentorship and guidance become indifferent to the things of the heart not because they are that heartless but because of lack of focus on the things of God with more focus on the things we want from God. In other words we need to relate to it and not cater to it. But some things we must confront not cater to because some things are destructive. But when offered with no consecration of heart it can be heady, hardy, and even nasty in its offering. That's why we seem to become more caring as we become weaker ourselves, needy and complete as we position ourselves in the complete image of God as men and women chosen vessels. Challenges create an environment for growth and maturity through need.

Challenge usually comes in your greatest weakness. JESUS' first teaching was you cannot put old wine in new wineskins. We can become stale and weakened by the skins we offer a new generation by not being malleable or flexible enough. People don't care how much you know till they know just how much you care. This is the lesson Paul reaches in Galatians 4 and this is the teaching of Jesus.

Again, let me say there are differences between men and women. God takes opposites and brings them together – but they didn't start as opposites but as one thing – called Adam. God out of the dirt made Adam but out of Adam he made Eve. Man and woman are supposed to complement each other because Eve is the part man does not have. Eve means man with a womb – it takes man and woman to form the complete part. Man and woman have been separated and with Focus they have to come back together now to make for a powerful vessel that God can use to fulfill promises. So what is the first thing the enemy does? He comes against their focus – their faith – obedience – commitment – unity – servant-hood. Continuing in this lack of focus still has no sensitivity to this challenge and it affects the purpose and promise of the church as we attempt to use our head and theological arguments instead of our hearts and focus on the things of God that bring us all together. That is what the enemy wants. He wants our rhetoric to separate us instead of loving one another as we come together in Christ to enjoy the grace, extend the glory and establish the throne that we might fulfill the promise.

Your worship is a part of this complete expression. Church is just a larger family made up of little families coming together. If the word doesn't work when it's tough it doesn't work at all. But when things get tough we must also become sensitive to people's weaknesses and challenges that God may be using to build up His body.

But again looking at the heart one must understand that as a chosen vessel we cannot operate in the kingdom and operate in the works of the flesh. When you look at (Galatians 5:19-21) this has to do with conduct/ behaviors.

<u>Flesh</u>	<u>Spirit</u>
Conduct/behaviors	attitudes (not conduct)

Paul is saying clean up your behavior and your attitudes for you are a chosen vessel for God's use.

Church people are obsessed with behavior and conduct and have some of the worst attitudes, and cold hearts one can ever imagine. Why is that? Holiness folk will examine someone's behavior and seem to never focus on their hearts. They would rather hide in your bushes to see what you're doing than spend time with you to see who you are. People calling themselves Christians, with telescopes are looking into your house to see about your conduct and behavior. They examine everything you did and who you did it with; to see if you ever did anything that they can judge you by.

Then the preacher contributes when he preaches that you can't do this or that. The church with its perspective of who is worthy and women cannot serve in leadership just adds to the perspective. Till your whole picture of God looks like a rule book! Since we can't keep his rules why try to have anything to do with him. So most of us run and some are stilling running even now; neither changing our behaviors, conduct or dealing with our attitudes and cold indifferent hearts.

Till one day we discover that God is not his rules and is okay regardless of how many rules of conduct people with bad attitudes offer you as an expression of who he truly is. Some of us would be better vessels for God if only we could get past some of the people we have run into in church. Tell the truth and curse the devil out of your life. You maybe judging God based on how some church people have been judging you and your perception of who you are in Christ is so distorted you believe that you are unworthy of being chosen by God to seek his perfect will for your life and to use you for his glory.

Have you ever wanted to invite someone to your house but you don't because you knew they would bring their children? How many houses has God never been invited into because people can't stand his children? The truth is that I, along with some of you, really, if the truth were known, would rather have people who were all messed up, behaviors and conduct all wrong, out of place and rejected by so-called church folk, but have a good attitude about God and what God can do. You can miss me however, when people come around that have never done anything wrong in their life and want to judge everybody with a judgmental attitude. They have never committed any sins, been a virgin till they were married, never said a cuss word or looked at anything or listened to any music that was perverted, or improper according to them. They have never let alcohol touch their lips, or used a drug of any kind. Their marriage is perfect, their children are perfect, they are more skilled and talented than anyone else and their friends even the unsaved ones are better than you and all your so-called friends put together.

Their momma was a saint, their daddy was god and they are angels on earth created to save and judge you. They'll tell you they have been walking in the way for thirty years yet they are judgmental as hell, critical, ugly spirited and self-righteous hypocrites. You judge everybody and have an opinion about everything, always causing division, strife and dissension. The fact is that you may never have done drugs or smoked cigarettes, drank alcohol or stole anything in your life and you might have been a virgin before you got married and never slept around but you are mean as hell and the bible says doing these things will make it so you will not inherit the kingdom of God.

Can you say . . . watch out church folk! We need to Focus and get some things right, not only in our behaviors but also in our attitudes which just may be the worst problem we have in the church; a lack of heartfelt and sensitive focus. I would rather lead a group of dysfunctional "use to be a lot of things" people who really in their heart loves God rather than folk who have been in church so long they can not even be used by God as vessels for his glory any longer. Jesus' first teaching was that you cannot put new wine into old rigid, inflexible, un-useable, wineskins. Why have all your flesh right but a spirit that sucks? No one wants to be around mean and ugly people for long. I know that I don't how about you?

Church we need to focus on getting a new attitude of gratitude as chosen vessels of God's grace. It is time to clean up the spirit of the church and our attitudes about her and one another. There comes a season in our spiritual lives when things that have worked for you in one season of life tend not to work any longer in a new season of your life. Things come through necessity to bring changes and there is a necessity even for your enemy to be of importance to your development if you can get past things like: betrayal, abandonment, challenges in ministry and judgments by people you love and depend on, which for some reason seem to all come up on you at one time and when it does can seem to paralyze you with fear, heady concerns or indifference to your own heart history and all but brings life to a stand still.

It is these things that most drain you emotionally and bring such a spirit of defeat into your life that you know you are at the point of either giving up or losing focus and change to find a Godly answer to what you are confronting. Beloved when you look at the Word of God from a different perspective, through a light of focus and understanding, with heart open to receiving God in it you begin to see in your desperation patterns that reveal God's plan and purpose for you. One of those revelations at this point in your journey begins to enlighten you to the fact that everyone who has ever done anything important in life, had an impact on their generation, overcame enemies, obstacles and challenges to their purpose and God's plan for them. The question is do you, as a chosen vessel of God for his glory, become discouraged when obstacles get in the way of your goal?

Do you get lost and lose your way and give up, give in to the enemy, obstacles, and challenges having lost heart in the pressure of the unfortunate attacks? It may very well be time for you to REFOCUS!

REmember, REvisit your first love, REstore your joy, REgard this present situation as part of your future glorification of what God will be able to trust you with when he chooses you for his glory; REcapture your perspective on life, love, longing, and laugher; REpay your debts, REvive your soul through prayer and fasting, REfocus on the word while openly without REstraint praise and worship God more sincerely and passionately, worship Him in spirit and in truth or in other words with head and heart as a chosen vessel of holiness.

A tread that seems to run throughout scripture is that one can't move ahead and get to your purpose, discover your destiny without moving mountains out of your way, overcoming giants, resisting the painful effects of obstacles like red seas, times of meandering through mazes of mediocrity in the wildernesses of life, drinking from the wells of bitterness, betrayal and venomous attacks before reaching your promised place in God. Sometimes your back may go out on you from the heaviness of the lift and your lung collapses through the strain of the struggle but you can't lose focus or lost heart in the battle.

Friends are usually there to comfort you. Family is there to keep one humble. But the truth is that enemies like Pharaoh for Moses; the Amalekites for the children of Israel; Saul for David; Hamon for Esther; those that would crucify Jesus and now you really are just there to promote you. Enemies are the ones that take us to places that without them, we would never have reached. What is prayer without pain sometimes to communicate through it your need for God's help? What is worship without adversity sometimes to focus it?

The Apostle Paul writes in I Corinthians 16:9 "There is a wide-open door for a great work here; although many oppose me." As believers we must focus and use common sense, pray without ceasing, study the word of God faithfully, and the situation fearlessly, seeking the best we can to determine the will of God. God gave us minds to think with, but he does not want us to rely strictly on our own reasoning when confronted by enemies, obstacles, or needed detours. We must pray, meditate on the Word, and even seek the Godly counsel of mature saints. In other words, we must REfocus. Our decisions even as chosen vessels may not always be in the will of God. We will make mistakes and make promises that we cannot keep and plans we cannot fulfill. The sin is to become hard hearted and running to flesh answers instead of standing firm in our faith and fidelity of focus.

Know that with great opposition, comes great opportunities. When one door seems to close and enemies oppose you, refocus because a wide-open door is somewhere in your future. Refocusing sometimes helps you get your power back through hope and understanding. When all hell breaks out on you, you tend to lose focus, hope and perspective; this is the strategy of the enemy. It is seemly to get you to lose focus and lose heart. It makes your heart sick and unable to go on through the difficulty it presents. David for example went from obscurity to popularity in one effort of focus on killing the giant that had come up against him and the promises of God for the lives of his people. What if God is using a giant problem to get you to faithfully confront that one enemy, obstacle or challenge that would take you from obscurity to notoriety and a season of fulfilled promise?

Our enemies, obstacles, situations, dry seasons, attacks and collapsed lungs are all keys to refocus our purpose and season of fulfilled promise in God as His chosen vessels. These things are signs that signal what the enemy is scared most about in your life that you would refocus and overcome it to reach your God-purposed destiny for His glory. Maybe you need to refocus and seek to understand just what this attack, obstacle or opposition is being using for to detract, discourage, or destroy your purpose and promise. When you lose hope through lack of focus the bible says your heart grows sick. Heart sick and hopeless affects the true quality and sense of fulfillment in life. In essence there is no life left because of a sick and hopeless heart.

Refocus dear one so that your heart can come to life again and you will desperately seek to fulfill the renewed desires of your heart. In the plan of God, victory comes through the overcoming of ones enemies, obstacles and challenges to your calling and the opposition to your wide-open doors for promise and purpose. Your condition and position sometimes are complete opposites. As a child of the most-high God you have privileges and an inheritance as royalty. You truly are a chosen vessel and you have rights and privileges to everything our father in heaven has. Consecrate yourself and present yourselves holy and acceptable unto God as your reasonable service and through Focus when God opens doors wide you then may step right into a season of fulfilled promises!

You are a Chosen Vessel

CONCLUSION

Our vision is to fulfill the Great Commission and the Great Commandment. Pleasing God and making disciples is the determining factor in everything the church ought to do. The strategy is to become a Sincere Church that loves with a pure heart, good conscience, and sincere faith (I Timothy 1:5) as we surrender, share, synergize, shape, and serve as disciples. Making disciples is helping people follow Jesus in all areas of life. While pleasing God is why we're here, we call it living the Christ-life!

Thus "Focus" becomes the essential process in accomplishing this sincere church goal, FOCUS as – faith – obedience – commitment – unity – servant-hood. Disunity in the church forms the greatest challenge to pleasing God, living the Christ-life and fulfilling the Great Commission to make disciples. When the church's focus is on the basic doctrines of the faith peripheral issues will not sidetrack us.

The Sincere Church is trying to grow people who think like the One who designed the stars, who astounded the rabbis, and who defeated the Pharisees; people who imagine the world like the One who wrote the parables; who make choices like the One whose meat and drink was to do the will of his Father; who serve like the One who took up a basin and towel and washed his disciples' feet; and who love like the One who died on Calvary.

J. Faraja Kafela

Biography

As a descendent of seven generations of <u>ministers, preachers, and men of God</u> in May 1998, Jelani Kafela answered the call to continue the legacy of dynamic visionary protectors and messengers of the gospel.

Jelani Faraja Kafela, now Bishop Kafela, whose name means "mighty hope for the future, for whom one has died" is the founding senior pastor of Imani Temple Christian Fellowship and the Presiding Prelate of the Bridge Network Covenant Fellowship of Associated Churches and Independent Ministries.

Bishop Kafela, a well studied and passionate Shepherd is also an author of two other prolific books 1) <u>Laugh Out Loud in the Face of Your Swagga Jackers</u> and 2) most recently released <u>Pursuing the Mystery of Perfection: Growing in Grace and Knowledge</u>.

Bishop Kafela in partnership with Promise Christian University has established the Shelter T. White Institute of Biblical Study (SWIBS) a certificate program for ministers and lay leaders. With over 40 active ministries, 22 ordained ministers, 18 Deacons and Deaconess along with the Imani Economic and Community Development Corporation, who's Invisible Hands Food Ministry feeds hundreds in the community each month.

Bishop Kafela has received the following honors:

- 13th Living History Award recipient, Jack and Jill, Inc.
- President's Award, NAACP, DES MOINES CHAPTER
- Community Service Award, National Black Child Development Institute
- Awarded Master "Hersetha" (Teacher) – The Institute for the Study of Black Family Life & Culture, Oakland CA (Dr Wade Nobles)
- Pastor of the Year, Inland Valley News
- Honorary Doctor of Divinity, Promise Christian University.

www.ingramcontent.com/pod-product-compliance
Lightning Source LLC
Chambersburg PA
CBHW061310110426
42742CB00012BA/2126